MINIATURE BULL T

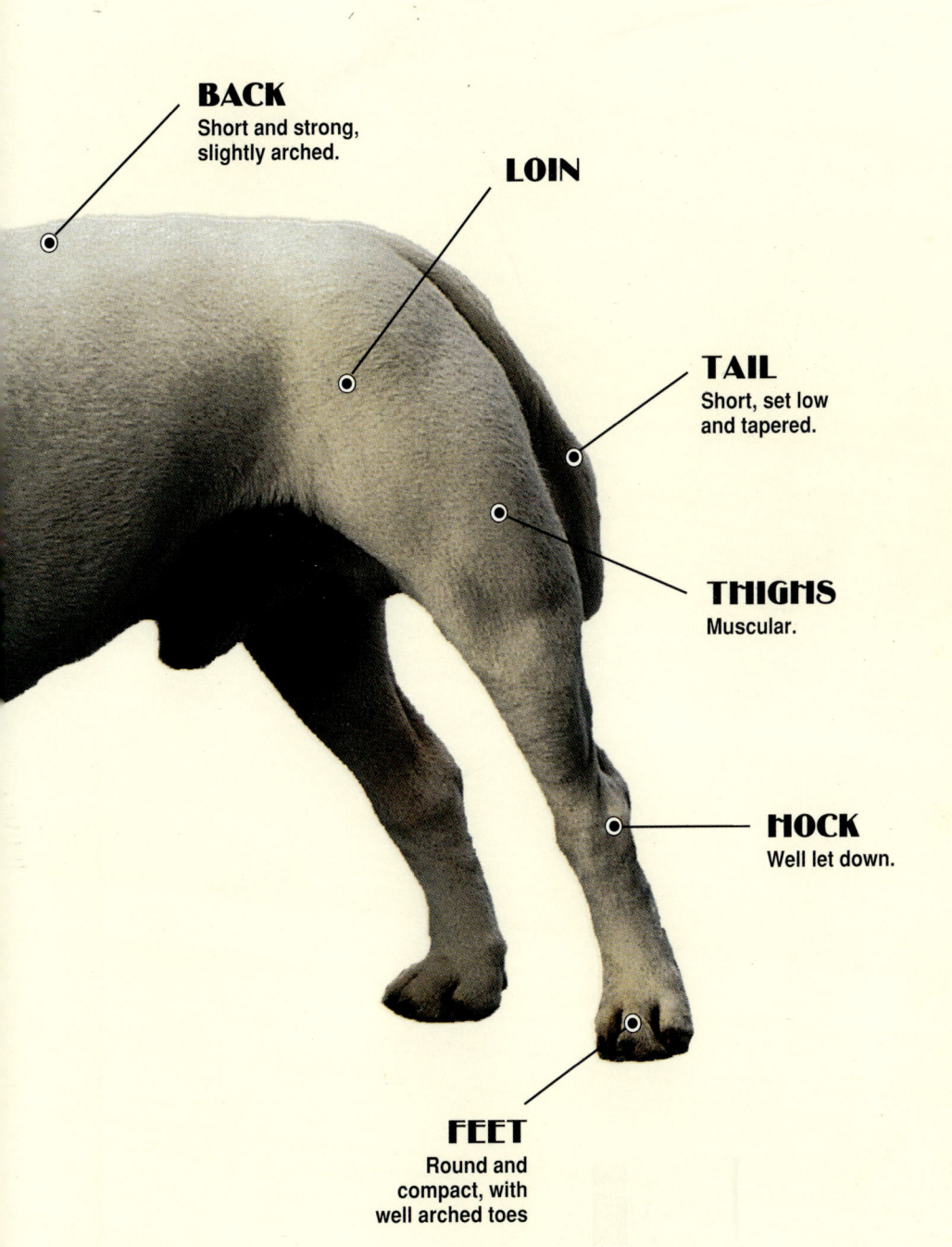

BACK
Short and strong, slightly arched.

LOIN

TAIL
Short, set low and tapered.

THIGHS
Muscular.

HOCK
Well let down.

FEET
Round and compact, with well arched toes

Title page: Miniature Bull Terrier owned by David and Susan Glasgow.

Photographers: Alverson Photographers, Inc., BJ and Bill Andrews, Cheryl Lynn Andrews, Ashbey Photography, Baines Photo, Mary Bloom, Booth Photography, Paulette Braun, Paul Combs, Wil de Veer, Isabelle Francais, David and Susan Glasgow, Pam and John Glave, Judy Iby, Kamala Dolphin-Kingsley, Marny Koch, the Otte family, Perry Phillips, Emily Russ, Susan Taylor, Michael M. Trafford.

© by T.F.H. Publications, Inc.

Distributed in the UNITED STATES to the Pet Trade by T.F.H. Publications, Inc., One T.F.H. Plaza, Neptune City, NJ 07753; distributed in the UNITED STATES to the Bookstore and Library Trade by National Book Network, Inc. 4720 Boston Way, Lanham MD 20706; in CANADA to the Pet Trade by H & L Pet Supplies Inc., 27 Kingston Crescent, Kitchener, Ontario N2B 2T6; Rolf C. Hagen Inc., 3225 Sartelon St. Laurent-Montreal Quebec H4R 1E8; in CANADA to the Book Trade by Vanwell Publishing Ltd., 1 Northrup Crescent, St. Catharines, Ontario L2M 6P5 ; in ENGLAND by T.F.H. Publications, PO Box 15, Waterlooville PO7 6BQ; in AUSTRALIA AND THE SOUTH PACIFIC by T.F.H. (Australia), Pty. Ltd., Box 149, Brookvale 2100 N.S.W., Australia; in NEW ZEALAND by Brooklands Aquarium Ltd. 5 McGiven Drive, New Plymouth, RD1 New Zealand; in Japan by T.F.H. Publications, Japan—Jiro Tsuda, 10-12-3 Ohjidai, Sakura, Chiba 285, Japan; in SOUTH AFRICA by Lopis (Pty) Ltd., P.O. Box 39127, Booysens, 2016, Johannesburg, South Africa. Published by T.F.H. Publications, Inc.

MANUFACTURED IN THE
UNITED STATES OF AMERICA
BY T.F.H. PUBLICATIONS, INC.

MINIATURE BULL TERRIER

A COMPLETE AND RELIABLE HANDBOOK

B. J. Andrews

RX-118

CONTENTS

Description of the Miniature Bull Terrier 7
Here's a Little Bull for You

Origin of the Minature Bull Terrier 15
The Beginning • The Brits Are Coming, The Brits Are Coming •
The Miniature Bull Terrier Club of America • The MBTCA Today •
Erenden Miniature Bull Terriers

Standard for the Miniature Bull Terrier 42

Your Puppy's New Home 46
On Arriving Home • Dangers in the Home • The First Night •
Other Pets • Housetraining • The Early Days • Identification

Feeding Your Miniature Bull Terrier 57
Factors Affecting Nutritional Needs • Composition and Role
of Food • Amount to Feed • When to Feed

Training Your Miniature Bull Terrier 65
Collar and Leash Training • The Come Command • The Sit
Command • The Heel Command • The Stay Command •
The Down Command • Recall to Heel Command • The No Command

Breed Concerns 74

Your Healthy Miniature Bull Terrier 78
Physical Exam • Healthy Teeth and Gums • Fighting Fleas •
The Trouble with Ticks • Insects and Other Outdoor Dangers •
Skin Disorders • Internal Disorders • Worms • Bloat
(Gastric Dilatation) • Vaccinations • Accidents

DESCRIPTION OF THE MINIATURE BULL TERRIER

HERE'S A LITTLE BULL FOR YOU

If you want a dog that chases Frisbees and butterflies—a dog who will play with boundless energy or sleep curled in your lap with immovable determination, well...think small. Actually, standard-sized Bull Terriers will do the same things, but they will not fit in your lap as well.

The Mini-Bull fits into compact cars and loves convertibles. He is never in the way in a small apartment and is a fitting doorman for the most expansive estate. He's a dog who is ready for anything, anytime. His fiercely comical face gets him into the best places and like the gentleman he was bred to be, he's always welcomed back.

The Miniature Bull Terrier's sweet and loyal personality is matched by his strength and determination. Adult and pup owned by David and Susan Glasgow.

DESCRIPTION

He will entertain you for hours. His comedy repertoire is limitless and he will laugh at himself right along with you. When the excitement is over, however, it's as though you switched him off. He will curl up beside you, preferably on the sofa, and tucking his head face-down under his chest, he'll snuggle contentedly for hours.

Does the Mini-Bull get along with other dogs? A common question from people who are familiar with their background. Bull Terriers are very much like people. They like some dogs and don't like others. Ours were inseparable, moms even raised each other's pups and adult males were quite tolerant of youngsters, male or female. Minis try to be polite and if the other dog is friendly, there will seldom be a problem. If the other dog behaves in an aggressive manner, then yes, there will probably be a problem. One must ensure that strange dogs do not take liberties.

What are Mini-Bulls like to live with? There could be no better example than one of this author's first

A natural comedian, the Mini Bull will provide his owner with a lifetime of entertainment. Ch. Erenden Ephraim, or "Effy," owned by the author, cracks himself up.

DESCRIPTION

English imports. Ephraim was extremely shy when he came to America. He had suffered a terrible table experience as a puppy, the end result being a bad fall after an examination that had degenerated into a wrestling match. Had his breeder not thought him ruined for the ring, my husband Bill and I would probably not have been able to acquire the dog at all.

Bill took "Effy" under his protection but was determined to make a Bull Terrier of him! He made a point of smacking Effy from behind and the dog soon

Who is this little devil? Behind this innocent expression, Ch. Crescent T.K.O has been known to "raise Cain" occasionally.

learned to actually *expect* to be surprised, whacked on the buttocks, or lifted by the tail. He was not allowed to cringe, for in so doing, he was quite likely to find himself being dragged along on his belly and being a smart boy, he quickly decided that was no fun.

Effy soon graduated to the job of truck-partner and he proudly took on the uncharacteristic role of car guard because his boss expected it. One of Bill's plumbers nearly lost his cool and his hand when sent to fetch a tool from the truck. He may have caught Effy napping on the job but it took only a split second for the dog to become a roaring white tornado!

His favorite game (the dog's I should state, although Bill invented it) was to crouch down behind a

9

DESCRIPTION

Miniature Bull Terriers enrich the lives of their owners by being loving and faithful companions. Pete and Julia Otte with Ch. Terezija Von Furstengraben.

few blades of grass and there to lie in wait for some unwitting canine passerby. Of course Bill went along with it by squatting down beside the dog, whispering man-stuff like "watch 'em" and "here they come Buddy." Effy would cast worried looks at Bill's exposure—obviously he considered himself well hidden. Loving Bill so much, he allowed him to participate even at the risk of giving away their position. Good-natured guy that Effy was, he never seemed to resent being restrained from actually jumping at the unsuspecting dog. Of course the people could see Bill and Effy "hiding" and the approaching dogs were unconcerned by their presence. So Effy was always convinced that he had ambushed an unsuspecting quarry and it delighted him to no end. Shy? No, not after three months of red-neck fun.

Are Mini-Bulls good with children? Well, one might ask, are the children good with dogs? If the dog is treated with kindness and respect, then yes, rare is the Mini-Bull who won't consider a child as his very best friend and bedfellow.

Are Mini-Bulls good watchdogs? No. Well, perhaps a male might be protective of his family or his automobile but generally speaking, the Bull Terrier, Mini or Standard, would likely welcome company even in the middle of the night as long as the family is not there. If the visitor wants the silver, the Bullie knows exactly where it's kept and will probably escort the thief to it. It should be noted however that only a very brave (or blind) burglar could possibly intrude past the face of a Bull Terrier! He would either be frightened by the wicked expression and the massive frontal bone and

DESCRIPTION

head shape—or laugh so loudly someone would be sure to call the cops!

Are Mini-Bulls destructive? Well, not really. There is something about feather pillows that appeals to all canines, but most Mini-Bulls would prefer to lounge on pillows rather than destroy them. I should warn you though that if the pillow should move on its own, it does become fair game. If they are taught early on that table legs are not for the purpose of cutting one's teeth and televisions are to be watched, not defended against, there is usually no problem. Vacuum cleaners may, however, be considered oversized and overly noisy varmints (i.e. rats) by Mini-Bulls. The laundry basket is seldom at risk, indeed it is perceived as an ideal bed for the "home alone" Mini. After all, it smells the most like his loved one and while he might occasionally take an undergarment along while checking on that noise at the front door, he's to be forgiven for an inability to do two things at once!

And what about housebreaking you ask? Well, the biggest difficulty might be in removing him from your lap long enough to insist that he perform necessary toilet routines. And it can be a bit of a pain convincing

Who can resist a sleeping Mini? A Mini Bull is happiest when he's snuggling with the ones he loves. Owned by David and Susan Glasgow.

DESCRIPTION

a sleepy Mini that he should go outside in the rain to empty out before bedtime. The true "relief" here is knowing that the capacity of a Bull Terrier's stomach is exceeded only by his bladder.

If you are overly concerned about having a fully obedient dog, get another breed. The Mini-Bull often marches to a drummer you will never hear—but you will laugh at the cadence he keeps! Even when he's being "disobedient" he is so appealingly innocent it is difficult to be annoyed at his antics.

Effy once grabbed up a two-by-four board about eight feet long. The strength of the breed is amazing but Effy's cleverness at testing out the right center of

Although small in size, the Miniature Bull Terrier is a true "muscle man," possessing great strength and endurance. Ch. Crescent T.K.O. shows his weight-lifting abilities.

balance had us so entranced that we didn't think to stop him until he actually took off with his prize. Then realizing the danger to yard furniture and the other dogs, we began yelling for him to "drop it." Lips pulled back from his strong white teeth, he seemed to be laughing at us as he sailed by with the heavy board held high. Grace and Elly, our other dogs, spotted him and decided to charge him from the other side. "Oh no," groaned Bill as the three dogs converged. Effy saw Grace and swung the board to keep his treasured new toy away from her. He did not see Elly, but Elly saw stars! Unaware of the downed dog in his wake, he bounded on across the yard. We saw the second wreck coming as he raced between the corner of the porch and the pine tree.

DESCRIPTION

The Mini Bull's unique appearance and charming ways win him admirers wherever he goes! Three-month-old Classic Dreams Anna Pavlova owned by Janis Dolphin and Cheryl Gutzivilek.

Poor Effy. He continued to love balls and squeakies — soft, safe toys — but he never again played with sticks.

The Mini-Bull is 20 to 30 pounds of rock hard muscle wrapped in a tough tight hide, which in whites is endearingly pink! Being so "muscle bound," his movement is not the flowing gait of many herding or working dogs—it is more suited to that of any Olympic weight lifter. He runs as he's built, with the most charming, awkward, side-kicking, utter abandon and joyousness of a donkey first turned out to pasture after a long hard winter!

He requires absolutely no special grooming or care. He is the ultimate "sport utility vehicle," an indestructible four wheel drive, with just a smidgen of chrome for contrast!

Fortunately for all who have been captivated by the corky little guy that is the Miniature Bull Terrier, be

DESCRIPTION

assured, he is not a dwarf and he has very few of the problems associated with miniaturization.

The hands of many great dog people in England and America have shaped the development of the Miniature Bull Terrier over the last century. Owners are as intensely and fiercely devoted to their dogs as are the dogs to their people. The Bull Terrier, Miniature or Standard, is as unique in his character and loveability as he is in his appearance.

So if you want a comedic, entertaining, infinitely loyal companion that will be socially acceptable just about anywhere; if you want a comfortable bed mate who never makes demands on you; if you aspire to the unusual and don't mind being engaged in conversation every time you walk your dog; if you have no desire to coddle a pet and not much time for grooming chores; if your space is limited or you drive a one-seater convertible; and if you are willing to risk your heart to one of the most utterly charming animals developed by man to serve man—then by all means, purchase a Miniature Bull Terrier!

If you are looking for a low-maintenance dog with a great sense of humor, the Miniature Bull Terrier is the breed for you! Owner, P. Goppel.

ORIGIN OF THE MINIATURE BULL TERRIER

THE BEGINNING

The Miniature is everything the standard-sized Bull Terrier is, only smaller. Because the two are inseparable, one must understand the beginnings of the Bull and Terrier breeds in order to fully appreciate the Mini-Bull.

The Bulldog of the mid-1800s was still a pretty ferocious canine, having descended from the infamous dogs bred during the reign of King John (1209) for the sport of bull-baiting and subsequently for other blood sports.

The first breed standard for the Bulldog was not written until 1865 and it described a dog "very rare" and "very mistreated, and as a rule, very poorly understood." Indeed, that first standard clearly defines the Bulldog as "an animal of the nation, com-

To fully appreciate the Miniature Bull Terrier, one must understand the journey the breed has taken from street fighter to family pet.

ORIGIN

pletely identical with Old England—it is a dog that every Englishman can be proud of." Dog fighting was officially outlawed in England in 1935 and the Bulldog could have become extinct except for his own notorious tenacity and that of those who loved him and refused to allow him to fade into obscurity.

Even as the fighting Bulldog began to undergo the inevitable modification that has made him such a wonderful family companion, the enterprising dog breeder Mr. James Hinks was experimenting with crosses involving the now extinct English White Terrier. It was this gentleman, about whom so little is known, who first put the Bull and Terrier on the map—Birmingham, England to be precise. He is said to have begun creating the Bull and Terrier even as dog fighting came into debate, and one might speculate that he did so with a rather nefarious purpose in mind. By the early 1850s, Mr. Hinks had it just about right and he presented an exciting new dog that he officially dubbed the Bull and Terrier.

Today's aversion to blood sports would have us look the other way rather than confront the actual history of the blood brother to the Mini-Bull. Despite the official decree, dog fighting continued although it moved to the back alleys and became a sport no longer associated with the upper class. But make no mistake, the Bull and Terrier that preceded the accomplished hand of Mr. Hinks was a fighting dog par excellence! One very famous dog called Trusty was often written up in *Sporting Magazine* during the year 1804. Due to his fighting ability, the 42-pound dog was sold many times during his career, each time for higher sums. At one time he was owned by the famous boxing champion, Jem Belcher and it was said that only an undefeated man was worthy of owning such an unbeatable dog.

Of the new Bull and Terrier type, Stonehenge writes, "When bred in this way, the Bull and Terrier is the fighting dog par excellence, and in actuality there is scarcely a task that you could use a dog of this size for that it could not do just as well, far better, than others." Pierce Egan, a sporting events commentator, said of the Bull Terrier, "This new breed is without doubt highly suitable as a life's companion for active, venturesome young men...."

Mr. Hinks is credited with correcting the rather roached back and stiff back legs of the Bulldog while also setting a fairly level bite instead of the steely

Opposite: Successfully crossing the Bull and Terrier with the White English Terrier led to the creation of the first White Bull Terrier. An original painting by Cheryl Lynn Andrews of Ch. Erenden Ephraim owned by Bill and BJ Andrews.

ORIGIN

ORIGIN

undershot grip of the bull-baiter. His design was to serve two purposes, and fortunately, the breed's prowess in the pits eventually gave way to a demand for a stylish show dog and steadfast family friend. By 1860, the breed had pretty well split into the pure-white Bull Terrier and the old colored Bull and Terrier dogs who were still pit-fighting in the shadows, who finally emerged as Staffordshire Bull Terriers.

The Bull Terrier does not deny his heritage nor his success as the ultimate gladiator of the fighting pits any more than he gets squeamish about quickly dispatching a hundred rats tossed into the same pit. Our British friends, so quiet, so well mannered, were known for more than a stiff upper lip. They were men of steel and even today, the ladies (including the Royals) are proving to be made of stern stuff. And so it was that the pure-white Bull Terrier became the stylish pet of prominent English gentlemen. The titled gentry began to take serious interest in the former

The Bull Terrier was created by English fanciers and quickly became a symbol of Britain's unyielding ingenuity. A Bull Terrier owned by Jim and Kathy Cavanaugh.

ORIGIN

Once a fighting dog, the pure-white Bull Terrier eventually became a stylish pet of the English gentry. White Mini Bull Terriers owned by David and Susan Glasgow.

back alley ruffian and he quickly became known as the "White Cavalier."

That moniker led to greater demand for the all-white color as the utmost fashion statement. This sent our entrepreneurial Mr. Hinks back to work creating a dominant white specimen. By the 1860s he had succeeded with what became the prototype of the breed. He rigidly culled the piebald pups, breeding white to white except for a small dash of Dalmatian blood to set the overall white body and perhaps to add a bit of stylish shape. An earlier infusion of Spanish Pointer contributed leg length and size.

The Bull Terrier became a well made, agile, strong and intensely loyal companion of the upper class. He was in fact, bred by gentlemen for gentlemen, sporting men who still enjoyed the occasional proving of who had the toughest dog. The Bull Terrier was therefore expected to be a gentleman, one who should never start a fight but felt it was perfectly all right to defend oneself! Indeed, the Bull Terrier was expected to do so and to willingly give his blood in defense of his reputation—or that of his owner!

With this in mind, we can safely assume that Mr. Hinks and others began to concentrate on appearance as much as on fighting ability despite the popular

ORIGIN

saying "a handsome gladiator who can not hold his sword and shield ably is soon a dead gladiator."

So it was when Hinks was rudely braced by some chaps who chided him about the lack of fighting spirit in his "pretty" dogs, he matched his 40-pound female "Puss" against the 60-pound dog of one Mr. Tupper. Mr. Tupper's dog was soundly trounced and, as though to rub salt in the wounds Mr. Hinks then trotted Puss off to win a red ribbon that same day at the Holborn dog show! Although that fitting end to the episode has been questioned, who is to say what sort of grooming standards were demanded or whether or not the judge had already heard of Puss's earlier work of the day?

On a more modern note, one of the most famous Bull Terriers was Willy, General George Patton's dog. Although Willy was said to be gun shy, loyalty decreed he ride next to the General, even into the field of battle. And where Willy might have been nervous around heavy cannon, he once took a firm grasp on a French diplomat's trouser leg and was known for his bravery and corky attitude. The absolute steadfastness and unwavering devotion of the breed has never been more poignantly captured than in the award-winning photo of Willy waiting to go home with his master's remains.

As the Bull Terrier breed evolved, deafness became problematic as did other genetic evidence of the efforts to maintain an all-white dog developed from a limited gene pool. The "commonness" of the brindle color was spurned until it was realized that many genetic assets were hidden in the dark pigment. Even so, breeders of colored Bull Terriers had a rough go of it until a Miss Montague Johnstone finally achieved success with her Romany Kennel. Although the colored and the whites are still shown separately, a white-carrying brindle is very desirable and the same is true in the smaller size gladiator. The backwardness and fetish-like beliefs of 19th century Bull Terrier breeders should serve as a red flag to those who would put color or dentition or markings or anatomical faults above overall breed type, temperament and health! Were it not for leaders such as Raymond Oppenheimer, common sense and a true understanding for the fragility of proper breed type might have never become the by-word of successful Bull Terrier fanciers.

Opposite: The devotion and fortitude of the Bull Terrier is illustrated in Life *magazine's portrait of General George Patton's dog, Willy, waiting to go home with his master's belongings.*

ORIGIN

Snuggled up against the belongings of his late master, General Patton's dog Willie waits to be shipped home

ORIGIN

ENTER THE MINIATURE

According to English authorities, the Miniature and Toy sizes were developed by crossing the old English Toy Terrier, the black and tan, and "various dwarf specimens bred from full-sized parents," and the "small" size dogs were "bred mainly for sporting purposes." The "night of Neat's benefit" in November 1821 advertised a famous 18-pound fighting bitch and there are many other references to fighting dogs of 6 to 20 pounds during the period from 1820 to 1850. Records from the Kennel Club (England) Stud Book, First Volume indicate that small Bull Terriers were quite numerous, and in fact, the first recorded Bull Terrier Champion weighed less than 16 pounds! He was whelped in 1866 and recorded in the stud book as #2758 Nelson. His breeder was Mr. J. Willock, and he was owned Mr. S.E. Shirley from Stratford-on-Avon.

Toy Bull Terriers were first listed at the Great International Dog Show on May 25, 1863 where they were specified as "under 10 pounds in weight." These tiny dogs were difficult to breed, both as an achievement of type and from a reproductive standpoint. By 1883 the "small class" limit was raised to under 25 pounds, and for a period, Toy Bull Terriers were in great favor as overall health and vitality improved.

Even so, very tiny Toy Bull Terriers continued to be admired and Lady Evelyn Ewart, who herself owned a winning Toy named Tiny Mite, wrote in 1906 "Pony Queen, the property of Sir Raymond Tyrriott Wilson, weighed under 3 lbs. when full grown."

T.W. Hogarth's book on the Bull Terrier quotes Mr. Theo Marples's article in *Our Dogs,* May 1908: "The breed is divided into three main weights—viz. heavy, medium, and toy." In another excerpt, we learn a valuable point when considering any variety wherein the size has been reduced. Type as it relates to the larger size is often difficult to maintain in the smaller package and Mr. Marples nails it quite nicely in stating, "The great difficulty in the toys is to get good heads and fronts, and where a toy excels in these two important properties he should be given extra credit for them, and in breeding they should be aimed at more than any other."

The Toy Bull Terrier continued to enjoy favor in England and there was a small following in the States until the AKC ruled in 1916 that Winner's Classes

Opposite: Miniature Bull Terriers were originally shown as Toy Bull Terriers under the Bull Terrier breed. Author BJ Andrews and four-month-old Shurlock Holmes O'BJ.

ORIGIN

ORIGIN

would not be provided until numbers increased. Other breeds affected by this ruling were the Bedlington Terrier and the Boxer. The last year Toy Bull Terriers were exhibited at Westminster was 1922.

Many wonder at the demise of the Toy Bull Terrier and others wonder if, in fact, the very tiny dogs really disappeared at all or if, as the demand for more exaggerated heads increased, the little Toy with faults described as "round skulls, weak faces, poor tail carriage, and inferior conformation" became too lacking in type to be considered a proper Bull Terrier.

Mr. Glyn makes reference to dwarfs being produced from full-sized parents that had much better heads but he also cautions that Toy blood contributes to a "tendency to apple heads, goggle eyes and snipey muzzles." There have been reports even today of "runts" appearing in Miniature litters but, unfortunately, they are usually destroyed and the breeders prefer not to discuss what most would consider as a genetic defect. It might be interesting to preserve some of these tiny pups to see what they look like at maturity! With today's genetic mapping technology and the overall advancements in the complex art of matching up faults and virtues, the reappearance of a true Toy variety with acceptable breed type is a possibility and would offer a stimulating challenge to master breeders.

The first decade of the 20th century still presented much variance in size and shape, but the Miniature variety was defined as 12 pounds by the year 1914. Again the weight limit seems to have been the undoing of typy toy-sized Bullies and by 1918 the Miniatures were in decline and Toys were practically extinct. The weight limit was then raised to 18 pounds, which allowed fanciers of the smaller sizes to refresh the gene pool. That seemed a turning point in England and again the breed flourished, even including a few good Toy specimens.

Mr. Shirley, the first chairman of The Kennel Club (of England) himself had a large kennel of small Bull Terriers weighing less than 16 pounds. And so it was that The Miniature Bull Terrier Club Of England was founded in 1938. The Chairman was Richard H. Glyn who saw to it that the first "small" Bull Terriers became registered as Miniatures in 1939.

Continuing to breed standard to miniature-sized dogs has been the salvation of the Miniature although

ORIGIN

Conscientious breeders have strived throughout the years to retain the Mini Bull's good qualities.

the Toy size had all but vanished. Roger de Foblanque quotes Mr. Shirley as stating in 1903, "I have not seen a Bull Terrier for ten years to be compared with the old fashioned little ones." The AKC does not allow size interbreeding but The Kennel Club and the Australian Kennel Club periodically open the stud book to allow the varieties to be bred back and forth for reasons of genetic health.

No one is quite sure why so many Brits liked the smaller size. Some say that it was a handy size for a working ratter but it may be that the smaller variety was preferred by the ladies and perhaps by those who sought to counteract the ever-increasing size of the Bull Terrier. Whatever the reason, the smaller sized Bullie hung fast to the hearts and the imagination of all dog lovers.

If the English liked moderate sizes, it would seem that "big" was the preference of Americans. The last year Miniature Bull Terriers were exhibited at

ORIGIN

The Mini Bull was admitted to the Miscellaneous Class in 1963 and the Miniature Bull Terrier Club was formed in 1966.

Westminster was 1928 and the variety did not come back into favor until May of 1961 when Mrs. Ralph Gordon imported English Ch. Navigation Pinto and Freesail Simone. The Mini was either relegated or admitted (depending on one's point of view) to the Miscellaneous class in 1963.

The California-based Miniature Bull Terrier Club was formed in 1966. Larry and Jackie McArthur (Imperial Kennels) were quite active, showing in both California and Mexico. Larry served as the President of the small club for many years but the MBT failed to gain AKC breed status. It was a "catch-22" situation. The low numbers in the US prevented the breed from moving into regular competition and a gradual deterioration of quality due to the limited gene pool further decreased interest...and numbers.

Even though there were such outstanding examples in England as Eng. Ch. Kirbeon Bandmaster, by the early 1980s, the Miniature version of the Bull Terrier had become little more than a memory in the US. Although the McArthurs still owned Minis, there had been no functioning club for over a decade and there was very little interest in a breed that had degenerated into a weedy, shallow, common-headed, unsound dog as compared to the fabulous Standard Bullies of

ORIGIN

the day. Mention the "Miniature" and Bull Terrier breeders either raised questioning eyebrows or indignantly responded "there's no such thing!"

THE BRITS ARE COMING, THE BRITS ARE COMING

This author had become enchanted with the Bull Terrier in the mid-seventies and purchased three show-quality dogs from Banbury and another top kennel. The breeding program that had by then produced over 100 AKC Champion Akitas turned for a brief time to Bull Terriers. Three carefully bred litters produced Group, Specialty, and Westminster winners in Standards but my husband began to think about something smaller.

Great Bull Terriers such as those presented by Jim and Maggie Burns (Iffinest), Chris and Pat Dresser (Dress Circle), Mary and Jay Remer (Bedrock), Dave Merriam (Broadside), Matthew and "Winkie" Mackay-Smith (Banbury), Drue King (Westbrook), Marilyn Drewes (Nippys) and many other outstanding breeders made the insufficiencies in Minis harder to accept. Indeed the Mini-Bull in America as a competitive and uniform breed did not exist.

Still, we became convinced that a truly good Bull Terrier in a smaller size was a worthwhile goal, and so we decided to take on the challenge.

An outstanding example of an English Miniature Bull Terrier, Eng. Ch. Kirbeon Bandmaster.

ORIGIN

And a challenge it was. There was only one place to go if one wanted a true Bull Terrier in a smaller package. This author had seen examples of quality on a judging trip to England and was blessed with two valuable assets—-determination and the assistance of Mrs. Meg Purnell-Carpenter. It was Meg's standing in the dog community as a Championship show judge, popular columnist, and a true "dog lady" that enabled us to acquire several exceedingly good dogs from England.

The English are notably reluctant to part with top breeding stock and even when willing, the purchase

One of the first four Mini Bulls to arrive in the United States from England's Erenden Kennels, Erenden Fergus owned by Pam Glave.

price and shipping costs can be prohibitive for all but the most ardent enthusiast. While that was as true in the early 80s as it is today, we and the Glaves set out to revive the Mini in the US.

After nearly a year of searching and negotiating, the first Miniature Bull Terriers were personally flown to O'BJ Kennels by Meg Purnell-Carpenter. They were from the small but very successful Erenden kennel of Mrs. Valerie Allenden. It was a momentous occasion in the history of the Miniature Bull Terrier and the dogs themselves lived up to the moment. They were of outstanding quality, a tribute to their breeder and a delight to their new owners.

ORIGIN

Those first four arrivals were 14-month-old litterbrothers, both Crufts qualified and BIS puppies, Erenden Felix and Erenden Fergus. Meg, being the breeder's breeder, had also managed the purchase of two wonderfully compatible four-month-old litter sisters, Erenden Grace and Erenden Greta. The hard-won imports were shared with trusted friends, Pam and John Glave.

We asked Pam to record her view of the breed's rebirth in America. With the wonderful sense of humor for which she is so well known, Pam writes:

"Shortly after I met BJ in 1972, she held an obedience class which I attended. Being the only two people with Akitas in our part of Virginia, we became fast friends—-and still are 25 years later. At that class, a couple brought their Mini-Bull puppy. BJ and I had never seen a Mini Bull and even though the pup turned obedience into a new comic art form, we were smitten. They had purchased him in California and did not remember from whom.

"My husband John and I looked for years and never found a Mini Bull. Even though they were in Miscellaneous and had been since 1966, we never saw one. Since we could not find a Mini Bull we bought a standard Bull Terrier from BJ who had not been able to wait for a Mini either.

"Miss Piggy was a delight and lived compatibly with my Akitas and German Shepherds for almost 13 years. She finished easily, won BOB at a large Specialty and got a Group I but was better loved for her

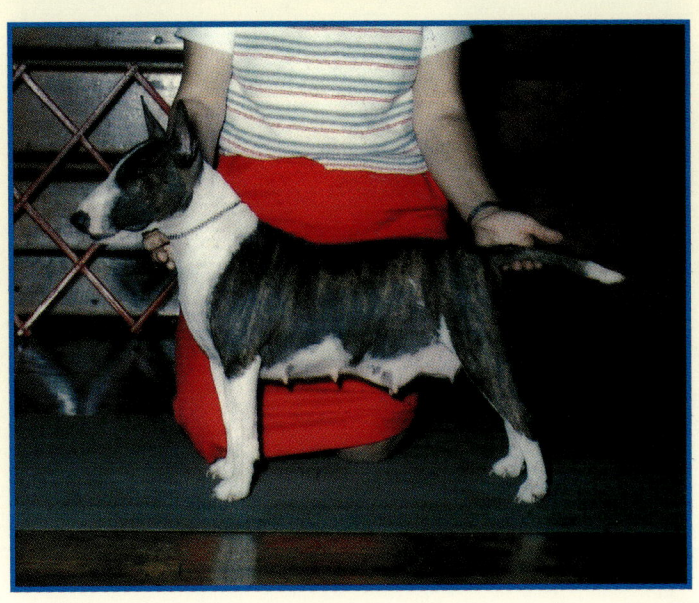

Erenden Greta, owned by Pam Glave, was one of the first Mini Bull bitches to be imported from England.

ORIGIN

other skills. She would retrieve anything—from bricks to carpet lint—and she once put a rocking chair through the wall while chasing a ball! We *definitely* still wanted a Mini (smaller holes in the wall) and when BJ (other than my husband, the most tenacious person I know) finally located a breeder in England, we were able to acquire our first "smaller" Bull Terrier.

"Valerie Allenden of Erenden Mini Bulls sent litter brothers Fergus and Felix and the two litter sisters, Erenden Grace and Erenden Greta. BJ had her pick of the males and took Felix so I got pick bitch and took Greta.

"Greta was the one perfect dog everyone gets once in their lifetime, if they are lucky. She was small, had nice type, was an excellent mom and was known all over the East as 'the Ambassador of the Breed.' She attended many shows where she built up a considerable fan club—Greta sang and danced for everyone. Many people were converted to Mini Bull fanciers because of Greta's wonderful temperament.

"Fergus, on the other hand, was not imported from England—he was exported to America! On the way

Eng. Ch. Erenden Elenore, imported by Bill and BJ Andrews and owned by Tam Cordingly.

home from BJ's house, we stopped at a rest area on the interstate. My friend Susan went to get Fergus out of his crate just as the people in the car next to us took out their Poodle. Susan was holding him in the air by his collar and tail and Fergus was roaring and swearing nonstop. The poor man with the Poodle yelled 'What is That?' I replied 'A chainsaw!' We can laugh at this now but Fergus was a trial all his life. I have always suspected BJ somehow knew this and picked Felix over Fergus."

The British dogs were so impressive that the Andrews immediately began negotiations for the purchase of the first English Champion import, Erenden

ORIGIN

The British Miniature Bull Terriers were deemed so impressive that the author arranged for the import of the first English champion, Erenden Elenore.

Eleanore and her outstanding white litter brother, Erenden Ephraim. Elly was placed with Tam Cordingly, a Terrier breeder and licensed handler. With the continued assistance of Meg Purnell-Carpenter and the breeding expertise of Valerie Allenden, the Andrews built a nucleus of top quality breeding stock in the US and Canada. Bill and BJ imported over a dozen outstanding dogs and by judiciously placing them with serious breeders, the breed was 'off and running' in the States."

THE KENNEL CLUB

This is to certify that
Mr. & Mrs. E. & V. Allenden's Bull Terrier(Miniature)
ERENDEN ELEANOR
has qualified for the title of
CHAMPION
under Kennel Club Rules and Regulations

30th August, 1983

1 Clarges Street
PICCADILLY
LONDON W1Y 8AB

Signed
Executive Officer

THE MINIATURE BULL TERRIER CLUB OF AMERICA

Pam Glave was co-founder of the new club and shares those memories with us:

"The beginning of my love for Mini Bulls was also the beginning of the MBTCA. I have always said BJ was a 'mover and a shaker' and nothing illustrated this better than the restoration of the MBTCA. The original club had died out and the majority of the records were lost in a hurricane in Mississippi. In 1983, BJ called me and said 'we're going to restart the Mini Bull Club.'

"'Right,' I thought. I had two children, 15 dogs, a full-time job, and my husband was on a submarine and gone for nine months. 'Sure,' I said—you cannot say no to BJ's enthusiasm. She had called some other people who were interested in Mini Bulls and they had

ORIGIN

also pledged help, that would have been Janet Rothard, Linda Jensen, and a handful of Bull Terrier people.

"We were scattered all over the country but we did a great job forming the club. When my husband came home, he started the club newsletter '*A Little Bull*.' He and I wrote and printed the newsletter for some time before Robert Powell took over.

"A little over two years later we had our first National Specialty in conjunction with the BTCA Silverwood competition. The show was held October 1985 in the ballroom of the Atlanta Ramada, or maybe it was the Hyatt. Winkie MacKay Smith judged a great entry with people coming from as far away as California. Jackie McArthur, a member of the original MBTCA, was able to come and we eagerly pumped her for historical and breed information. Betty Carrol from California was also there with Justeph Country Man 'Patch' who is in a lot of our pedigrees today. John and I showed Erenden Greta and Erenden Fergus and two of their puppies. BJ and Bill showed Erenden Ephraim and Erenden Grace. Ephraim (Effy to his friends) was the second best male but Gracie won the Breed with Zedbees Zarkinson going BOS after having become dreadfully ill during the last moments of judging.

"As the years went on, more and more people became enchanted with Minis and the Club grew until we were recognized in 1991.

Erenden Ephraim O'BJ, owned by Bill and BJ Andrews, is considered an outstanding example of the breed. He took second place at the first Mini Bull specialty in the US.

ORIGIN

Imarii's Sister Mary Agnes, pictured with Pam Glave, was the first Miniature Bull Terrier bitch to get a Group placing.

"Quality and type have definitely improved over the years. Our first Minis were sometimes lacking in both. At first, the English breeders were reluctant to sell us their best, I think. Over the years this has changed as they have seen we can breed good ones too!"

After extensive consultation with AKC Executive Secretary Mark Mooty, this author reorganized the long-defunct club, serving as both President and Executive Secretary. The Miniature Bull Terrier Club of America was small but blessed with the following founding officers: Linda Jensen, Vice President; Pamela Glave, Treasurer; and John Glave as the first editor of *"A Little Bull."*

33

ORIGIN

Formal elections were held in 1985 and the Constitution and Bylaws were brought under revision. The stud book was also partially restored from scraps of information remaining after a flood had washed away previous archives and records. New registration forms and club pedigree records were designed and pieces of the previous club history were slowly and painstakingly put together.

The first "Specialty" show was arranged to be held in conjunction with the Bull Terrier Club of America show October 19, 1985. The judge for such an important "first" had to be not only qualified in the breed but someone who truly cared about the Bull Terrier in all sizes. AKC judge Mrs. Winkie Mackay-Smith graciously accepted. Of that historic occasion, Winkie writes:

"I feel very honored to have been asked to judge the first Miniature Bull Terrier Match Show and enjoyed myself immensely. It is very exciting to participate in the inception of the organization of Miniatures in this country and the entry bodes well for the success of the Miniatures both in numbers and quality."

The Best Puppy was Lucky Lucy Of Wilko (by Warbonnet Red Rum x Justeph Hurricane Girl) owned by Pattie and Ross Vorhees. The Best In Match (BB) was Erenden Grace O'BJ (Torigonina Adam x Erenden Clara) owned by BJ Andrews and handled by Mary Remer of Bedrock fame. Best Opposite Sex was Zedbees Zarkinson (Eng. Ch. Zedbee's Zedtozee x Zedbee's Zerica) owned by R.G. Beauchamp and F. Cazier.

Through concerted "PR" efforts, the breed began to generate interest. I called upon my friends and Bull Terrier breeders and they liked what they saw. O'BJ was campaigning the Number One Akita during the mid-eighties and, like a comic book parody of Mary Had a Little Lamb, everywhere that big dog went, his friends were sure to go. The powerful black Akita and his odd entourage of Mini Bulls drew well planned attention to a breed so enchanting and so *lovable* that although people came out of curiosity, most left with love and ownership plans!

Judges and Bull Terrier breeders who began the litany of "well, they aren't *really* Bull Terriers...." always stopped cold when Bill Andrews walked up with the white dog Erenden Ephraim. His soundness, his oh-so-corky attitude, and his incredible head took the words away from those with such antiquated opinions.

ORIGIN

This continued exposure to top show breeders and the judging community paid off. Mr. E.W. Tipton, one of the most highly respected All-Breed judges, became a stalwart champion of the breed. His favorite was Effy and many is the judge who will remember "Tip" encouraging them to "come see this dog." AKC Representative (now popular AKC judge) Mrs. Constance Barton was known to generously look the other way when we walked our unentered, non-AKC dogs on the show grounds. After all, who was to say they were not just small Bull Terriers? Certainly the quality was on a par with the best Standards!

Little by little, then by leaps and bounds, the Mini-Bull became the new darling of the show crowd. Shurlock Holmes O'BJ, a homebred from our first litter, was an exceedingly stylish youngster. His flashy color, soundness, and the exceptional turn and finish of his head brought many new devotees to the breed.

A puppy from the author's first litter bred in the US, three-month-old Shurlock Holmes O'BJ shows the signs of greatness to come.

Mr. Richard Beauchamp, publisher of Kennel Review Magazine and international judge, was also known for bringing new breeds to the forefront. He had been a major force in moving the Bichon Frise into full AKC recognition, so BJ promptly enlisted his help on behalf of the Mini-Bull and appointed Richard to the MBTCA Board of Directors.

Kennel Review and Carnation Company jointly sponsored the most exclusive and glamorous dog show in America. The *Tournament of Champions* was just that, a unique showcase for the creme de la creme of America's show dogs. The event was staged (in the truest sense of the word) the weekend of the famous Detroit Kennel Club shows at Cobo Hall. The Preliminary Competition took place all day with the

ORIGIN

winners being brought forward to the evening Finals amidst the glitter of the elaborate and very formal dinner party.

There, competing with the top Nationally ranked dogs and their famous handlers, strutted one corky little terrier and a very nervous owner-handler. Bill and I had contracted to videotape the event, so not revealing ourselves as breeders, we insisted that Shurlock Holmes O'BJ be shown by my novice co-owner. Having defeated many challengers in the Preliminaries, Shurlock moved forward to the exciting evening competition escorted by his ever-more bewildered novice co-owner. The Finals are judged by a panel of three top judges, and the impact the little Mini-Bull's win had on the bejeweled assemblage of famous owners and celebrities was electric! The stage-struck handler didn't have to "show" Shurlock, he showed himself! He posed and strutted, captivating the judges right along with ringside.

Another moment in history was written. As Rare Breed Finalist over a huge entry of Neos, Australians, PGVB, Dogue De Bordeaux, Lundhunds, Spinone, Couton and others too numerous to recall, the Miniature Bull Terrier prevailed. Heads were turned and minds were changed in the penthouse ballroom on that magical evening in 1986.

Shurlock and his parents, Gracie and Effy, were also appreciated by one of the country's top dog show photographers. Diana Alverson was and is among the best loved people in the sport and her enthusiasm for the "new" breed was boundless. Diana's generous professional skill was her gift to a breed she loved!

Winkie MacKay-Smith and Mary Remer both became ardent supporters of the Mini. Other less secure Bull Terrier breeders were a bit worried, as well they might have been, for suddenly there was a growing number of "small" versions of the best Bull Terriers and they were correctly perceived as serious competition.

And so a debate was born. Separate breed or Variety? The controversy grew with fanciers splitting into two camps—those who wanted the Mini to have the genetic advantage of interbreeding with the Standard here in the US as was at that time done in England, and those who were stubbornly opposed on the grounds that it would somehow "destroy" the Standards! In actuality, many believe that the real

ORIGIN

resistance to accepting the Mini as a Bull Terrier Variety was a simple reluctance to compete against them!

The breed grew in numbers even as the debate on how to apply for stud book status heated up. The immature behavior of a growing number of Mini-Bull owners was having its effect on those who had worked so hard to establish the breed in the US. A disgusted Richard Beauchamp resigned from the MBTCA Board of Directors and I grew more and more to regret having failed to follow Richard's advice, which was to limit the Board to those with solid experience in the sport until such time as the breed had achieved the goal of AKC recognition. I had created positions and unwittingly filled them with people who began to put political aspirations ahead of their love for the dogs.

Ch. Shurlock Holmes O'BJ puts the Miniature Bull Terrier on the map by making the finals in the Rare Breed division at the 1986 Tournament of Champions.

ORIGIN

An Erenden Kennel litter of Miniature Bull Terriers bred by English breeder Valerie Allenden.

The honeymoon was over. The Miniature had arrived but his unprecedented popularity carried a price. The expanded MBTCA Board was fussing amongst itself with the sad result that even the election process was corrupted that year. Having experienced too much bickering in the Akita breed and unable to bring rationality and common sense to the increasingly heated discussions, I resigned as President.

Despite the shadow cast by a handful of mercenary people, the Mini made it out of Miscellaneous in 1991 and by the mid-nineties, thanks to the steadying hand of experienced Bull Terrier fanciers, breed quality was exceeding that of the early 80s and the Parent Club had recovered nicely.

THE MBTCA TODAY

We asked President Paul Combs to provide an overview of the club to which he graciously responded:

"The Miniature Bull Terrier Club of America, like the breed, has gradually evolved. In the 1980s the Miniature Bull Terriers were shown in the Miscellaneous Class with ILP numbers.

"On October 1, 1991 Miniature Bull Terriers were officially recognized and admitted to the AKC. Miniature Bull Terriers were able receive championship points at AKC show beginning January 1, 1992.

"On October 12, 1992 the Van Hildrikhuesen Trophy Competition began. The Van Hildrikhuesen show is a competition for the Best-American Bred Miniature

ORIGIN

Bull Terrier. The bronze perpetual trophy was donated by Ziselotte Frank of the Van Hildrikhuesen Kennel of Germany. The Van Hildrikhuesen Trophy Show is held in conjunction with the MBTCA and its breeders are making a concerted effort to improve the quality, health, and well being of Miniature Bull Terriers.

"The Club encourages testing for genetic health problems, participating in health seminars, careful selective breeding, and Breed Rescue. Breeders make every effort to find the best homes for their puppies but sometimes Mini Bulls end up in the need of rescue."

ERENDEN MINIATURE BULL TERRIER
by Valerie Allenden

In 1966, when I became a "lady of leisure" and finished working, Eric and I decided that we could now have a dog. We were both from families where there had been dogs, so it was an inevitability. We decided

From the famous Zedbees Kennels, where Mrs. Valerie Allenden bought her first Mini Bull, Ch. Kearby's Mini Mo carries on the tradition of greatness.

ORIGIN

that we would like to have Bloodhounds, and so our adventures into pedigree dogs, showing and breeding began. After two children and several Bloodhound litters, Eric said that he would like a small dog to compliment the hounds, although he was not sure what he wanted. It had to be small, but not a "sissy" dog—in other words, not a pretty toy dog. After much searching and asking thousands of questions, we at last found the breed we wanted. Unfortunately it was difficult to get a puppy at that time, as there were only really two breeders producing any puppies in quantity. They were Mrs. Berry (Zedbees) and Mr. and Mrs. Kirby (Kirbeon). Eric had a birthday coming up and I had the good fortune of getting him a puppy, Zedbees Zhat, from Mrs. Berry in 1974. This was the start of a love affair that has not stopped. We bred our first litter

ERENDEN
Miniature Bull Terriers

Ch ERENDEN WHISKY SANGAREE, JW

We wish our many friends at home and abroad a very Merry Christmas and a Happy and Successful New Year

ERIC and VALERIE ALLENDEN
42 Pontac Road, New Marske
Redcar, Cleveland TS11 8AW
Telephone 0642 472824

Eng. Aust. Ch. Erenden Whiskey Sanagree, Junior Warrent Winner, is a wonderful representation of the Mini Bull Terriers produced at Erenden Kennels.

ORIGIN

Australian Ch. Erenden Roxana, a Miniature Bull Terrier bred by Erenden Kennels.

in 1975 and although we found them a difficult breed after the hounds, we were determined not to be beaten and kept on trying. We bred our first champion Erenden Eleanor in 1981, by Ch. Beewau Enterprise out of Erenden Caroline. She was a lovely red and white who we later sold to Mrs. B.J. Andrews in the United States. Unfortunately, the breed was not recognized in time for her to be seen at the shows where she would have undoubtedly gained her US title. Ch. Erenden Leopold by Curraneye Yoohoo out of Erenden Gertrude came in 1984. He was a real little bully and produced some very nice offspring for us. In 1987, we mated Erenden Gin Rickey to Erenden Tiny Tuggem and produced English and Australian Ch. Erenden Whiskey Sangaree. Over the years we bred approximately 200 Minis, some 25 of which have found their way to America. Some were brought as pets and others have been used in breeding programs throughout the country.

In 1993, Eric had a couple of heart attacks and in 1994 he passed away. As my mother was now living with me, I could not continue with my breeding programs as I would have wished and am only now beginning to get things going again. Hopefully, the Erenden Kennels **will be back.**

STANDARD FOR THE MINIATURE BULL TERRIER

A standard is a written description of the "ideal dog," a dog that in actuality has never existed and never will. The following standard is the approved standard of the American Kennel Club, the principal governing body for the dog sport in the United States. The standard is drafted and proposed by the national parent club, and then accepted by AKC. As the parent club sees fit, the standard can change from time to time, though these changes are essentially quite minor, usually pertaining to the format of the standard itself or perhaps some word choice. Studying the breed standard will reveal much about the dog itself, its character, and its ideal physique. Whether you are interested in breeding, showing, or just enjoying your Miniature Bull Terrier, the standard makes required reading for any breed fancier.

One of the first Mini Bulls to become a champion after breed recognition, Ch. Hobbit Hills Sir Winston, owned by Susan Taylor, wins Best of Variety.

STANDARD

General Appearance—The Miniature Bull Terrier must be strongly built, symmetrical and active, with a keen, determined and intelligent expression. He should be full of fire, having a courageous, even temperament and be amenable to discipline.

Size, Proportion, Substance—*Height*—10 inches to 14 inches. Dogs outside these limits should be faulted. *Weight* in proportion to height. In *proportion,* the Miniature Bull Terrier should give the appearance of being square.

Head—The *head* should be long, strong and deep, right to the end of the muzzle, but not coarse. The *full face* should be oval in outline and be filled completely up, giving the impression of fullness with a surface devoid of hollows or indentations, i.e., egg shaped. The *profile* should curve gently downwards from the

The Miniature Bull Terrier should be the embodiment of strength, alertness and substance. Ch. Crescent Saladin owned by Marny Koch.

top of the skull to the tip of the nose. The *forehead* should be flat across from ear to ear. The distance from the tip of the nose to the eyes should be perceptibly greater than that from the eyes to the top of the skull. The *underjaw* should be deep and well defined.

To achieve a keen, determined and intelligent *expression*, the *eyes* should be well sunken and as dark as possible with a piercing glint. They should be small, triangular and obliquely placed, set near together and high up on the dog's head. The *ears* should be small, thin and placed close together, capable of being held stiffly erect when they point upwards. The *nose* should be black, with well developed nostrils bent downwards at the tip. The *lips*

STANDARD

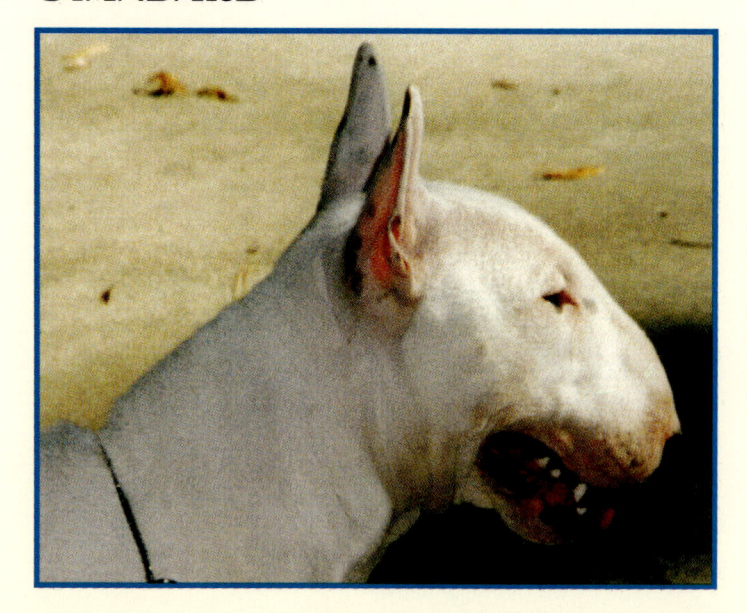

In accordance with the standard, the Mini Bull Terrier's head should curve gently downward to the tip of the nose. Ch. Greystone White On White owned by Paul Combs.

should be clean and tight. The *teeth* should meet in either a *level* or *scissor* bite. In the scissor bite, the top teeth should fit in front of and closely against the lower teeth. The teeth should be sound, strong and perfectly regular.

Neck, Topline, Body—The *neck* should be very muscular, long, and arched; tapering from the shoulders to the head, it should be free from loose skin. The *back* should be short and strong with a slight arch over the loin. Behind the shoulders there should be no slackness or dip at the withers.

The *body* should be well rounded with marked spring of rib. The back ribs deep. The *chest* should be broad when viewed from in front. There should be great depth from withers to brisket, so that the latter is nearer to the ground than the belly. The *underline,* from the brisket to the belly, should form a graceful upward curve. The *tail* should be short, set on low, fine, and should be carried horizontally. It should be thick where it joins the body, and should taper to a fine point.

Forequarters—The *shoulders* should be strong and muscular, but without heaviness. The shoulder blades should be wide and flat and there should be a very pronounced backward slope from the bottom edge of the blade to the top edge. The *legs* should be big boned but not to the point of coarseness. The *forelegs* should be of moderate length, perfectly straight, and the dog must stand firmly up on them. The *elbows* must turn neither in nor out, and the *pasterns* should be strong and upright.

STANDARD

Hindquarters—The *hind legs* should be parallel when viewed from behind. The *thighs* are very muscular with *hocks* well let down. The stifle joint is well bent with a well developed second thigh. The *hind pasterns* should be short and upright.

Feet—The *feet* are round and compact with well arched toes like a cat.

Coat—The *coat* should be short, flat and harsh to the touch with a fine gloss. The dog's skin should fit tightly.

Color—For white, pure white coat. Markings on head and skin pigmentation are not to be penalized. For colored, any color to predominate.

Gait—The dog shall move smoothly, covering the ground with free, easy strides. Fore and hind legs should move parallel to each other when viewed from in front or behind, with the forelegs reaching out well and the hind legs moving smoothly at the hip and flexing well at the stifle and hock. The dog should move compactly and in one piece but with a typical jaunty air that suggests agility and power.

Temperament—The temperament should be full of fire and courageous, but even and amenable to discipline.

Faults—Any departure from the foregoing points shall be considered a fault, and the seriousness of the fault shall be in exact proportion to its degree.

Approved May 14, 1991
Effective January 1, 1992

Ch. Hobbit Hills Elizabeth, owned by Susan Taylor, is shown here taking Best of Opposite Sex, and also has won multiple Best of Breeds.

YOUR PUPPY'S NEW HOME

Before actually collecting your puppy, it is better that you purchase the basic items you will need in advance of the pup's arrival date. This allows you more opportunity to shop around and ensure you have exactly what you want rather than having to buy lesser quality in a hurry.

It is always better to collect the puppy as early in the day as possible. In most instances this will mean that the puppy has a few hours with your family before it is time to retire for his first night's sleep away from his former home.

If the breeder is local, then you may not need any form of box to place the puppy in when you bring him home. A member of the family can hold the pup in his

When these Mini Bull puppies are ready to go to their new homes, they will need responsible owners to give them plenty of care and attention.

PUPPY'S NEW HOME

lap—duly protected by some towels just in case the puppy becomes car sick! Be sure to advise the breeder at what time you hope to arrive for the puppy, as this will obviously influence the feeding of the pup that morning or afternoon. If you arrive early in the day, then they will likely only give the pup a light breakfast so as to reduce the risk of travel sickness.

If the trip will be of a few hours duration, you should take a travel crate with you. The crate will provide your pup with a safe place to lie down and rest during the trip. During the trip, the puppy will no doubt wish to relieve his bowels, so you will have to make a few stops. On a long journey you may need a rest yourself,

How do you choose just one? Mini Bull puppies are adorable, so make sure you carefully consider the responsibility of pet ownership before taking one home. Owner, Paul Combs.

and can take the opportunity to let the puppy get some fresh air. However, do not let the puppy walk where there may have been a lot of other dogs because he might pick up an infection. Also, if he relieves his bowels at such a time, do not just leave the feces where they were dropped. This is the height of irresponsibility. It has resulted in many public parks and other places actually banning dogs. You can purchase poop-scoops from your pet shop and should have them with you whenever you are taking the dog out where he might foul a public place.

Your journey home should be made as quickly as possible. If it is a hot day, be sure the car interior is amply supplied with fresh air. It should never be too hot or too cold for the puppy. The pup must never be placed where he might be subject to a draft. If the journey requires an overnight stop at a motel, be

47

PUPPY'S NEW HOME

aware that other guests will not appreciate a puppy crying half the night. You must regard the puppy as a baby and comfort him so he does not cry for long periods. The worst thing you can do is to shout at or smack him. This will mean your relationship is off to a really bad start. You wouldn't smack a baby, and your puppy is still very much just this.

ON ARRIVING HOME

By the time you arrive home the puppy may be very tired, in which case he should be taken to his sleeping area and allowed to rest. Children should not be allowed to interfere with the pup when he is sleeping. If the pup is not tired, he can be allowed to investigate his new home—but always under your close supervision. After a short look around, the puppy will no doubt appreciate a light meal and a drink of water. Do not overfeed him at his first meal because he will be in an excited state and more likely to be sick.

Although it is an obvious temptation, you should not invite friends and neighbors around to see the new arrival until he has had at least 48 hours in which to settle down. Indeed, if you can delay this longer then do so, especially if the puppy is not fully vaccinated. At the very least, the visitors might introduce some local bacteria on their clothing that the puppy is not immune to. This aspect is always a risk when a pup has been moved some distance, so the fewer people the pup meets in the first week or so the better.

DANGERS IN THE HOME

Your home holds many potential dangers for a little mischievous puppy, so you must think about these in advance and be sure he is protected from them. The more obvious are as follows:

Open Fires. All open fires should be protected by a mesh screen guard so there is no danger of the pup being burned by spitting pieces of coal or wood.

Electrical Wires. Puppies just love chewing on things, so be sure that all electrical appliances are neatly hidden from view and are not left plugged in when not in use. It is not sufficient simply to turn the plug switch to the off position—pull the plug from the socket.

Open Doors. A door would seem a pretty innocuous object, yet with a strong draft it could kill or injure

PUPPY'S NEW HOME

Accustoming your Mini Bull to his crate not only makes housebreaking easier, it is the safest way for him to travel.

a puppy easily if it is slammed shut. Always ensure there is no risk of this happening. It is most likely during warm weather when you have windows or outside doors open and a sudden gust of wind blows through.

Balconies. If you live in a high-rise building, obviously the pup must be protected from falling. Be sure he cannot get through any railings on your patio, balcony, or deck.

Ponds and Pools. A garden pond or a swimming pool is a very dangerous place for a little puppy to be near. Be sure it is well screened so there is no risk of the pup falling in. It takes barely a minute for a pup—or a child—to drown.

The Kitchen. While many puppies will be kept in the kitchen, at least while they are toddlers and not able to control their bowel movements, this is a room full of

PUPPY'S NEW HOME

danger—especially while you are cooking. When cooking, keep the puppy in a play pen or in another room where he is safely out of harm's way. Alternatively, if you have a carry box or crate, put him in this so he can still see you but is well protected.

Be aware, when using washing machines, that more than one puppy has clambered in and decided to have a nap and received a wash instead! If you leave the washing machine door open and leave the room for any reason, then be sure to check inside the machine before you close the door and switch on.

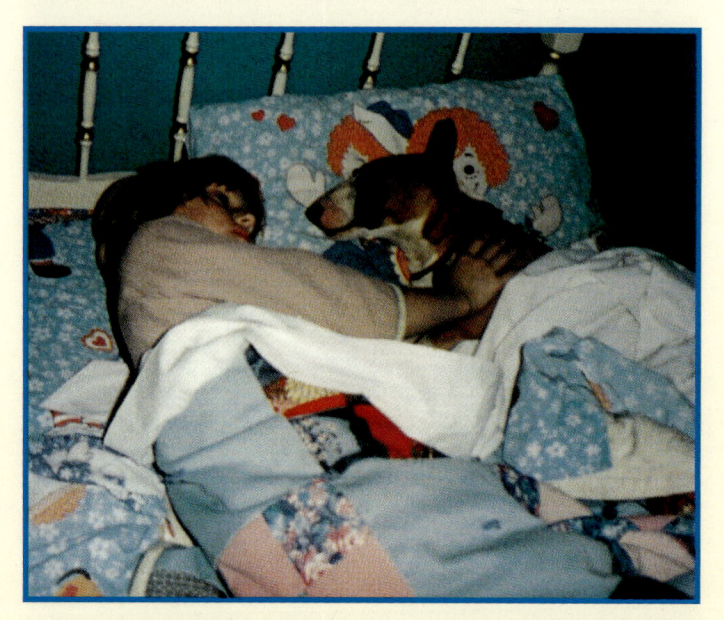

Children and Mini Bulls can be the best of friends as long as you educate your child on the proper way to handle dogs. Sally tries to kick her Mini friend Elly out of bed for snoring!

Small Children. Toddlers and small children should never be left unsupervised with puppies. In spite of such advice it is amazing just how many people not only do this but also allow children to pull and maul pups. They should be taught from the outset that a puppy is not a plaything to be dragged about the home—and they should be promptly scolded if they disobey.

Children must be shown how to lift a puppy so it is safe. Failure by you to correctly educate your children about dogs could one day result in their getting a very nasty bite or scratch. When a puppy is lifted, his weight must always be supported. To lift the pup, first place your right hand under his chest. Next, secure the pup by using your left hand to hold his neck. Now you can lift him and bring him close to your chest. Never lift a pup by his ears and, while he can be lifted by the scruff of his neck where the fur is loose, there is no reason ever to do this, so don't.

PUPPY'S NEW HOME

Beyond the dangers already cited you may be able to think of other ones that are specific to your home—steep basement steps or the like. Go around your home and check out all potential problems—you'll be glad you did.

THE FIRST NIGHT

The first few nights a puppy spends away from his mother and littermates are quite traumatic for him. He will feel very lonely, maybe cold, and will certainly miss the heartbeat of his siblings when sleeping. To help overcome his loneliness it may help to place a clock next to his bed—one with a loud tick. This will in some way soothe him, as the clock ticks to a rhythm not dissimilar from a heart beat. A cuddly toy may also help in the first few weeks. A dim nightlight may provide some comfort to the puppy, because his eyes will not yet be fully able to see in the dark. The puppy

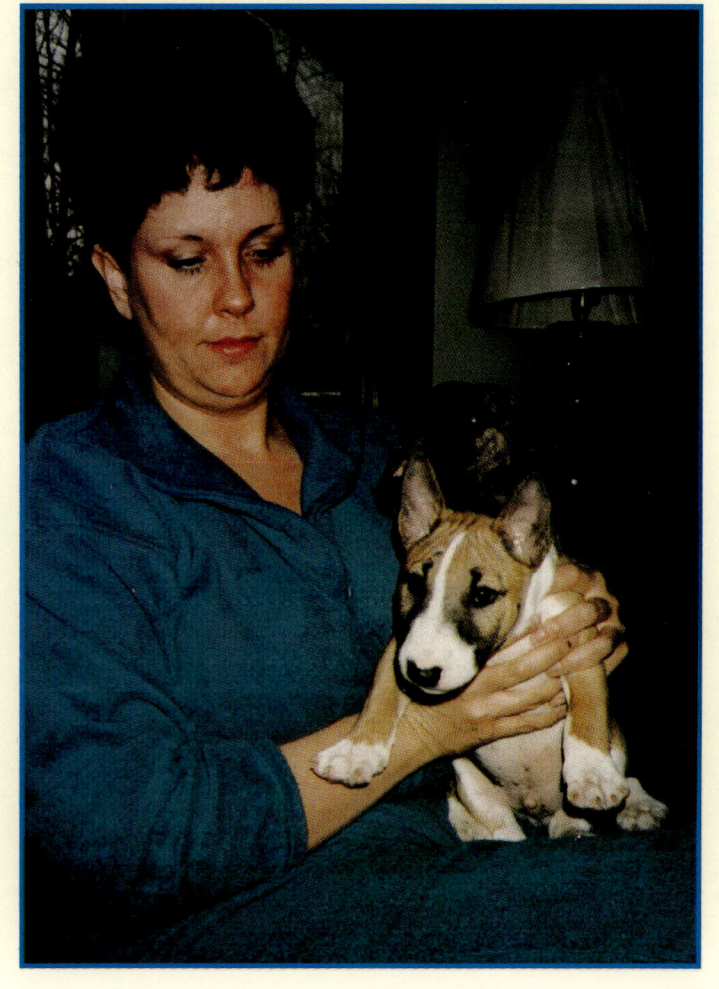

Your new puppy may miss the company of his littermates when you first bring him home, so try to make him as comfortable as possible. Debbie Lynch-Erlemeier and "Auntie Gracie" welcome an addition to the family.

PUPPY'S NEW HOME

may want to leave his bed for a drink or to relieve himself.

If the pup does whimper in the night, there are two things you should not do. One is to get up and chastise him, because he will not understand why you are shouting at him; and the other is to rush to comfort him every time he cries because he will quickly realize that if he wants you to come running all he needs to do is to holler loud enough!

By all means give your puppy some extra attention on his first night, but after this quickly refrain from so doing. The pup will cry for a while but then settle down and go to sleep. Some pups are, of course, worse than others in this respect, so you must use balanced judgment in the matter. Many owners take their pups to bed with them, and there is certainly nothing wrong with this.

The pup will be no trouble in such cases. However, you should only do this if you intend to let this be a permanent arrangement, otherwise it is hardly fair to the puppy. If you have decided to have two puppies, then they will keep each other company and you will have few problems.

OTHER PETS

If you have other pets in the home then the puppy must be introduced to them under careful supervi-

As long as they are properly introduced and carefully supervised, your Mini Bull Terrier should get along fine with other pets.

PUPPY'S NEW HOME

sion. Puppies will get on just fine with any other pets—but you must make due allowance for the respective sizes of the pets concerned, and appreciate that your puppy has a rather playful nature. It would be very foolish to leave him with a young rabbit. The pup will want to play and might bite the bunny and get altogether too rough with it. Kittens are more able to defend themselves from overly cheeky pups, who will get a quick scratch if they overstep the mark. The adult cat could obviously give the pup a very bad scratch, though generally cats will jump clear of pups and watch them from a suitable vantage point. Eventually they will meet at ground level where the cat will quickly hiss and box a puppy's ears. The pup will soon learn to respect an adult cat; thereafter they will probably develop into great friends as the pup matures into an adult dog.

Be patient and consistent when attempting to housebreak your puppy, as this is one of the first training tasks you will undertake together. Owners, Don and Emily Russ.

HOUSETRAINING

Undoubtedly, the first form of training your puppy will undergo is in respect to his toilet habits. To achieve this you can use either newspaper, or a large litter tray filled with soil or lined with newspaper. A puppy cannot control his bowels until he is a few months old, and not fully until he is an adult. Therefore you must anticipate his needs and be prepared for a few accidents. The prime times a pup will urinate and defecate are shortly after he wakes up from a sleep, shortly after he has eaten, and after he has been playing awhile. He will usually whimper and start searching the

PUPPY'S NEW HOME

room for a suitable place. You must quickly pick him up and place him on the newspaper or in the litter tray. Hold him in position gently but firmly. He might jump out of the box without doing anything on the first one or two occasions, but if you simply repeat the procedure every time you think he wants to relieve himself then eventually he will get the message.

When he does defecate as required, give him plenty of praise, telling him what a good puppy he is. The litter tray or newspaper must, of course, be cleaned or replaced after each use—puppies do not like using a dirty toilet any more than you do. The pup's toilet can be placed near the kitchen door and as he gets older the tray can be placed outside while the door is open. The pup will then start to use it while he is outside. From that time on, it is easy to get the pup to use a given area of the yard.

Many breeders recommend the popular alternative of crate training. Upon bringing the pup home, introduce him to his crate. The open wire crate is the best choice, placed in a restricted, draft-free area of the home. Put the pup's Nylabone® and other favorite toys in the crate along with a wool blanket or other suitable bedding. The puppy's natural cleanliness instincts prohibit him from soiling in the place where he sleeps, his crate. The puppy should be allowed to go in and out of the open crate during the day, but he should sleep in the crate at the night and at other intervals during the day. Whenever the pup is taken out of his crate, he should be brought outside (or to his newspapers) to do his business. Never use the crate as a place of punishment. You will see how quickly your pup takes to his crate, considering it as his own safe haven from the big world around him.

THE EARLY DAYS

You will no doubt be given much advice on how to bring up your puppy. This will come from dog-owning friends, neighbors, and through articles and books you may read on the subject. Some of the advice will be sound, some will be nothing short of rubbish. What you should do above all else is to keep an open mind and let common sense prevail over prejudice and worn-out ideas that have been handed down over the centuries. There is no one way that is superior to all others, no more than there is no one dog that is exactly a replica of another. Each is an individual and must always be regarded as such.

PUPPY'S NEW HOME

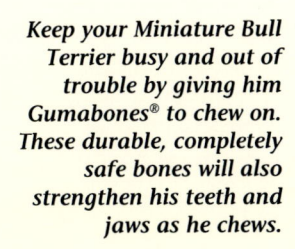

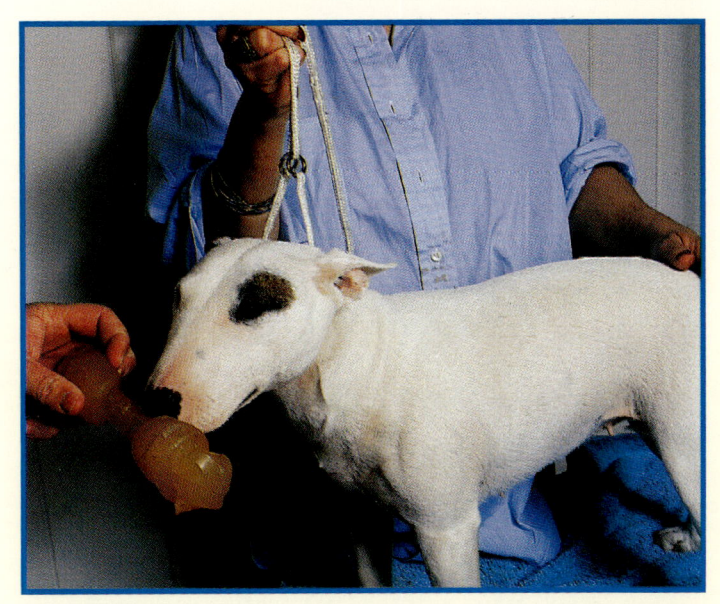

Keep your Miniature Bull Terrier busy and out of trouble by giving him Gumabones® to chew on. These durable, completely safe bones will also strengthen his teeth and jaws as he chews.

A dog never becomes disobedient, unruly, or a menace to society without the full consent of his owner. Your puppy may have many limitations, but the singular biggest limitation he is confronted with in so many instances is his owner's inability to understand his needs and how to cope with them.

IDENTIFICATION

It is a sad reflection on our society that the number of dogs and cats stolen every year runs into many thousands. To these can be added the number that get lost. If you do not want your cherished pet to be lost or stolen, then you should see that he is carrying a permanent identification number, as well as a temporary tag on his collar.

Permanent markings come in the form of tattoos placed either inside the pup's ear flap, or on the inner side of a pup's upper rear leg. The number given is then recorded with one of the national registration companies. Research laboratories will not purchase dogs carrying numbers as they realize these are clearly someone's pet, and not abandoned animals. As a result, thieves will normally abandon dogs so marked and this at least gives the dog a chance to be taken to the police or the dog pound, when the number can be traced and the dog reunited with its family. The only problem with this method at this time is that there are a number of registration bodies, so it is not always apparent which one the dog is registered with (as you provide the actual number). However, each registra-

55

PUPPY'S NEW HOME

tion body is aware of his competitors and will normally be happy to supply their addresses. Those holding the dog can check out which one you are with. It is not a perfect system, but until such is developed it's the best available.

Another permanent form of identification is the microchip, a computer chip that is no bigger than a grain of rice that is injected between the dog's shoulder blades. The dog feels no discomfort. The dog also receives a tag that says he is microchipped. If the dog is lost and picked up by the humane society, they can trace the owner by scanning the microchip. It is the safest form of identification.

A temporary tag takes the form of a metal or plastic disk large enough for you to place the dog's name and your phone number on it—maybe even your address as well. In virtually all places you will be required to obtain a license for your puppy. This may not become applicable until the pup is six months old, but it might apply regardless of his age. Much depends upon the state within a country, or the country itself, so check with your veterinarian if the breeder has not already advised you on this.

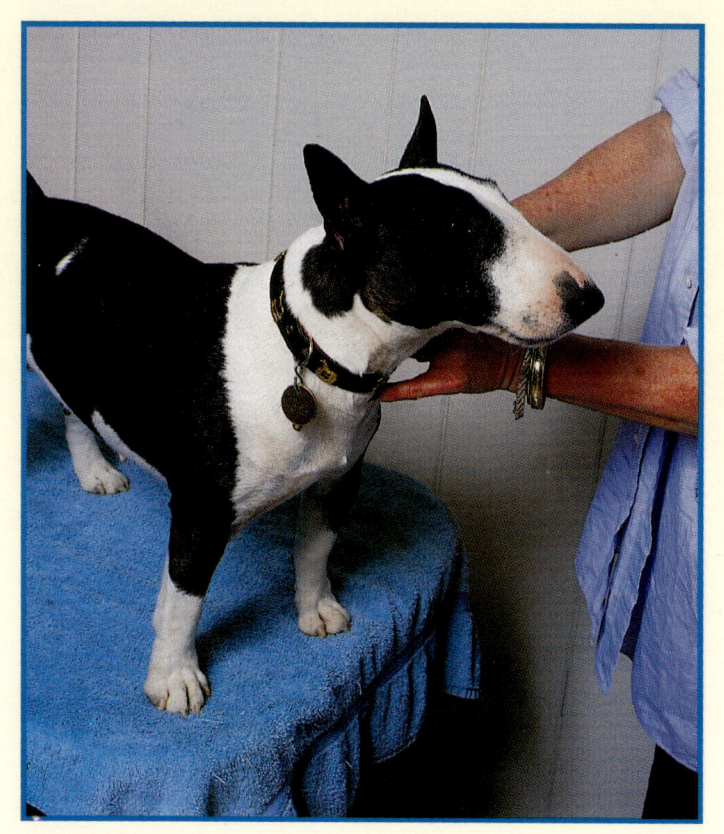

It is important that your Mini Bull wear a collar and identification tags at all times to increase the chances of his being returned should you become separated.

FEEDING YOUR MINIATURE BULL TERRIER

Dog owners today are fortunate in that they live in an age when considerable cash has been invested in the study of canine nutritional requirements. This means dog food manufacturers are very concerned about ensuring that their foods are of the best quality. The result of all of their studies, apart from the food itself, is that dog owners are bombarded

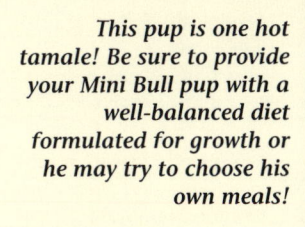

This pup is one hot tamale! Be sure to provide your Mini Bull pup with a well-balanced diet formulated for growth or he may try to choose his own meals!

with advertisements telling them why they must purchase a given brand. The number of products available to you is unlimited, so it is hardly surprising to find that dogs in general suffer from obesity and an excess of vitamins, rather than the reverse. Be sure to feed age-appropriate food—puppy food up to one year of age, adult food thereafter. Generally breeders recommend dry food supplemented by canned, if needed.

FEEDING

FACTORS AFFECTING NUTRITIONAL NEEDS

Activity Level. A dog that lives in a country environment and is able to exercise for long periods of the day will need more food than the same breed of dog living in an apartment and given little exercise.

Quality of the Food. Obviously the quality of food will affect the quantity required by a puppy. If the nutritional content of a food is low then the puppy will need more of it than if a better quality food was fed.

Balance of Nutrients and Vitamins. Feeding a puppy the correct balance of nutrients is not easy because the average person is not able to measure out ratios of one to another, so it is a case of trying to see that nothing is in excess. However, only tests, or your veterinarian, can be the source of reliable advice.

Genetic and Biological Variation. Apart from all of the other considerations, it should be remembered that each puppy is an individual. His genetic make-up will influence not only his physical characteristics but also his metabolic efficiency. This being so, two pups from the same litter can vary quite a bit in the amount of food they need to perform the same function under the same conditions. If you consider the potential combinations of all of these factors then you will see that pups of a given breed could vary quite a bit in the amount of food they will need. Before discussing feeding quantities it is valuable to know at least a little about the composition of food and its role in the body.

Carrots are rich in fiber, carbohydrates, and vitamin A. The Carrot Bone™ by Nylabone® is a durable chew containing no plastics or artificial ingredients and it can be served to your Mini Bull as-is, in a bone-hard form, or microwaved to a biscuit consistency.

FEEDING

COMPOSITION AND ROLE OF FOOD

The main ingredients of food are protein, fats, and carbohydrates, each of which is needed in relatively large quantities when compared to the other needs of vitamins and minerals. The other vital ingredient of food is, of course, water. Although all foods obviously contain some of the basic ingredients needed for an animal to survive, they do not all contain the ingredients in the needed ratios or type. For example, there are many forms of protein, just as there are many types of carbohydrates. Both of these compounds are found in meat and in vegetable matter—but not all of those that are needed will be in one particular meat or vegetable. Plants, especially, do not contain certain amino acids that are required for the synthesis of certain proteins needed by dogs.

Likewise, vitamins are found in meats and vegetable matter, but vegetables are a richer source of most. Meat contains very little carbohydrates. Some vitamins can be synthesized by the dog, so do not need to be supplied via the food. Dogs are carnivores and this means their digestive tract has evolved to need a high quantity of meat as compared to humans. The digestive system of carnivores is unable to break down the tough cellulose walls of plant matter, but it is easily able to assimilate proteins from meat.

In order to gain its needed vegetable matter in a form that it can cope with, the carnivore eats all of its prey. This includes the partly digested food

POPpups™ are 100% edible and enhanced with dog-friendly ingredients that your Mini Bull will love like liver, cheese, spinach, chicken, carrots, or potatoes. They contain NO salt, sugar, alcohol, plastic or preservatives. You can even microwave a POPpup™ to turn into a huge crackly treat.

FEEDING

within the stomach. In commercially prepared foods, the cellulose is broken down by cooking. During this process the vitamin content is either greatly reduced or lost altogether. The manufacturer therefore adds vitamins once the heat process has been completed. This is why commercial foods are so useful as part of a feeding regimen, providing they are of good quality and from a company that has prepared the foods very carefully.

Roar-Hide® is completely edible and is high in protein (over 86%) and low in fat (less than one-third of 1%). Unlike common rawhide, it is safer, less messy, and more fun for your Mini Bull.

Proteins

These are made from amino acids, of which at least ten are essential if a puppy is to maintain healthy growth. Proteins provide the building blocks for the puppy's body. The richest sources are meat, fish and poultry, together with their by-products. The latter will include milk, cheese, yogurt, fishmeal, and eggs. Vegetable matter that has a high protein content includes soy beans, together with numerous corn and other plant extracts that have been dehydrated. The actual protein content needed in the diet will be determined both by the activity level of the dog and his age. The total protein need will also be influenced by the digestibility factor of the food given.

Fats

These serve numerous roles in the puppy's body. They provide insulation against the cold, and help buffer the organs from knocks and general activity shocks. They provide the richest source of energy, and reserves of this, and they are vital in the transport

FEEDING

of vitamins and other nutrients, via the blood, to all other organs. Finally, it is the fat content within a diet that gives it palatability. It is important that the fat content of a diet should not be excessive. This is because the high energy content of fats (more than twice that of protein or carbohydrate) will increase the overall energy content of the diet. The puppy will adjust its food intake to that of its energy needs, which are obviously more easily met in a high-energy diet. This will mean that while the fats are providing the energy needs of the puppy, the overall diet may not be providing its protein, vitamin, and mineral needs, so signs of protein deficiency will become apparent. Rich sources of fats are meat, their byproducts (butter, milk), and vegetable oils, such as safflower, olive, corn or soy bean.

Provide your Miniature Bull Terrier with access to clean, cool water at all times.

Carbohydrates

These are the principal energy compounds given to puppies and adult dogs. Their inclusion within most commercial brand dog foods is for cost, rather than dietary needs. These compounds are more commonly known as sugars, and they are seen in simple or complex compounds of carbon, hydrogen, and oxygen. One of the simple sugars is called glucose, and it is vital to many metabolic processes. When large chains of glucose are created, they form compound sugars. One of these is called glycogen, and it is found in the cells of animals. Another, called starch, is the material that is found in the cells of plants.

Vitamins

These are not foods as such but chemical compounds that assist in all aspects of an animal's life. They

FEEDING

help in so many ways that to attempt to describe these effectively would require a chapter in itself. Fruits are a rich source of vitamins, as is the liver of most animals. Many vitamins are unstable and easily destroyed by light, heat, moisture, or rancidity. An excess of vitamins, especially A and D, has been proven to be very harmful. Provided a puppy is receiving a balanced diet, it is most unlikely there will be a deficiency, whereas hypervitaminosis (an excess of vitamins) has become quite common due to owners and breeders feeding unneeded supplements. The only time you should feed extra vitamins to your puppy is if your veterinarian advises you to.

Minerals

These provide strength to bone and cell tissue, as well as assist in many metabolic processes. Examples are calcium, phosphorous, copper, iron, magnesium, selenium, potassium, zinc, and sodium. The recommended amounts of all minerals in the diet has not been fully established. Calcium and phosphorous are known to be important, especially to puppies. They help in forming strong bone. As with vitamins, a mineral deficiency is most unlikely in pups given a good and varied diet. Again, an excess can create problems—this applying equally to calcium.

Water

This is the most important of all nutrients, as is easily shown by the fact that the adult dog is made up of about 60 percent water, the puppy containing an even higher percentage. Dogs must retain a water balance, which means that the total intake should be balanced by the total output. The intake comes either by direct input (the tap or its equivalent), plus water released when food is oxidized, known as metabolic water (remember that all foods contain the elements hydrogen and oxygen that recombine in the body to create water). A dog without adequate water will lose condition more rapidly than one depleted of food, a fact common to most animal species.

AMOUNT TO FEED

The best way to determine dietary requirements is by observing the puppy's general health and physical appearance. If he is well covered with

FEEDING

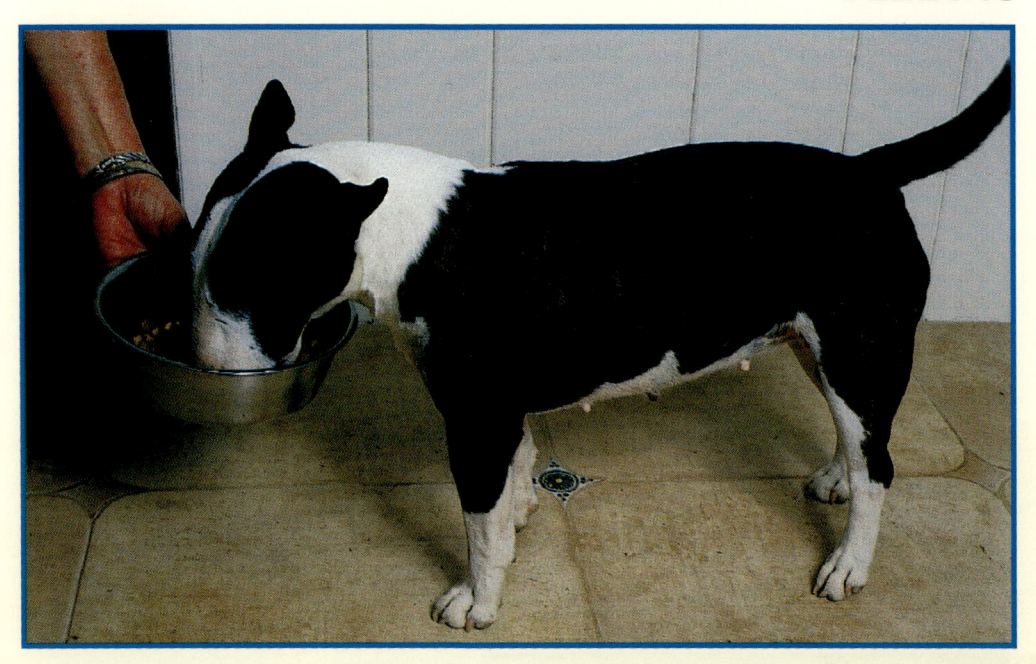

If you stick to a consistent feeding schedule, your Miniature Bull Terrier will always know when it is meal time.

flesh, shows good bone development and muscle, and is an active alert puppy, then his diet is fine. A puppy will consume about twice as much as an adult (of the same breed). You should ask the breeder of your puppy to show you the amounts fed to their pups and this will be a good starting point.

The puppy should eat his meal in about five to seven minutes. Any leftover food can be discarded or placed into the refrigerator until the next meal (but be sure it is thawed fully if your fridge is very cold).

If the puppy quickly devours its meal and is clearly still hungry, then you are not giving him enough food. If he eats readily but then begins to pick at it, or walks away leaving a quantity, then you are probably giving him too much food. Adjust this at the next meal and you will quickly begin to appreciate what the correct amount is. If, over a number of weeks, the pup starts to look fat, then he is obviously overeating; the reverse is true if he starts to look thin compared with others of the same breed.

WHEN TO FEED

It really does not matter what times of the day the puppy is fed, as long as he receives the needed quantity of food. Puppies from 8 weeks to 12 or 16 weeks need 3 or 4 meals a day. Older puppies and

FEEDING

adult dogs should be fed twice a day. What is most important is that the feeding times are reasonably regular. They can be tailored to fit in with your own timetable—for example, 7 a.m. and 6 p.m. The dog will then expect his meals at these times each day. Keeping regular feeding times and feeding set amounts will help you monitor your puppy's or dog's health. If a dog that's normally enthusiastic about mealtimes and eats readily suddenly shows a lack of interest in food, you'll know something's not right.

A nutritious diet will be evident in your Mini Bull's shiny coat, overall healthy appearance and winning smile! Owners, David and Susan Glasgow.

TRAINING YOUR MINIATURE BULL TERRIER

Once your puppy has settled into your home and responds to his name, then you can begin his basic training. Before giving advice on how you should go about doing this, two important points should be made. You should train the puppy in isolation of any potential distractions, and you should keep all lessons very short. It is essential that you have the full attention of your puppy. This is not possible if there are other people about, or televisions and radios on, or other pets in the vicinity. Even when the pup has become a young adult, the maximum time you should allocate to a lesson is about 20 minutes. However, you can give the puppy more than one lesson a day, three being as many as are recommended, each well spaced apart.

Before beginning a lesson, always play a little game with the puppy so he is in an active state of mind and thus more receptive to the matter at hand. Likewise, always end a lesson with fun-time for the pup, and always—this is most important—end on a high note, praising the puppy. Let the lesson end when the pup has done as you require so he receives lots of fuss. This will really build his confidence.

COLLAR AND LEASH TRAINING

Training a puppy to his collar and leash is very easy. Place a collar on the puppy and, although he will initially try to bite at it, he will soon forget it, the more so if you play with him. You can leave the collar on for a few hours. Some people leave their dogs' collars on all of the time, others only when they are taking the dog out. If it is to be left on, purchase a narrow or round one so it does not mark the fur.

TRAINING

Teaching your Mini Bull to wear his collar and leash is essential not only for his safety but for the safety of others. Owner, Mrs. Q. Youatt.

Once the puppy ignores his collar, then you can attach the leash to it and let the puppy pull this along behind it for a few minutes. However, if the pup starts to chew at the leash, simply hold the leash but keep it slack and let the pup go where he wants. The idea is to let him get the feel of the leash, but not get in the habit of chewing it. Repeat this a couple of times a day for two days and the pup will get used to the leash without thinking that it will restrain him—which you will not have attempted to do yet.

Next, you can let the pup understand that the leash will restrict his movements. The first time he realizes this, he will pull and buck or just sit down. Immediately call the pup to you and give him lots of fuss. Never tug on the leash so the puppy is dragged along the floor, as this simply implants a negative thought in his mind.

THE COME COMMAND

Come is the most vital of all commands and especially so for the independently minded dog. To teach the puppy to come, let him reach the end of a long lead, then give the command and his name, gently pulling him toward you at the same time. As soon as he associates the word come with the action of moving toward you, pull only when he does not respond immediately. As he starts to come, move back to make him learn that he must come from a distance as well as when he is close to you. Soon you

TRAINING

may be able to practice without a leash, but if he is slow to come or notably disobedient, go to him and pull him toward you, repeating the command. Never scold a dog during this exercise—or any other exercise. Remember the trick is that the puppy must want to come to you. For the very independent dog, hand signals may work better than verbal commands.

THE SIT COMMAND

As with most basic commands, your puppy will learn this one in just a few lessons. You can give the puppy two lessons a day on the sit command but he will make just as much progress with one 15-minute lesson each day. Some trainers will advise you that you should not proceed to other commands until the previous one has been learned really well. However,

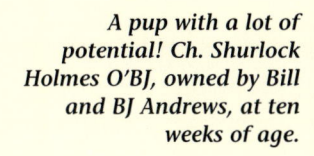

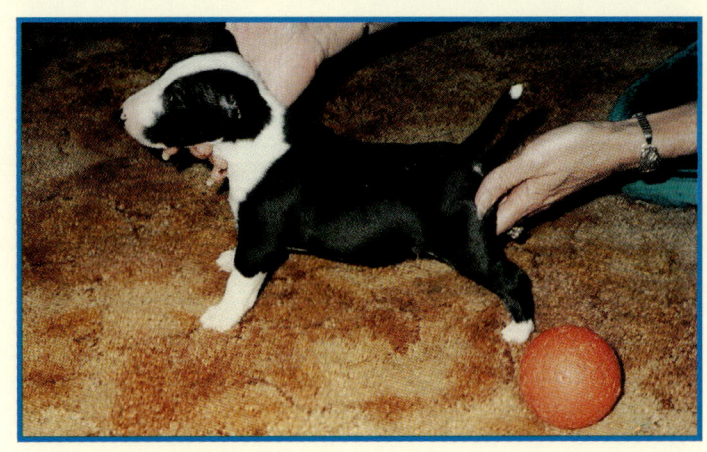

A pup with a lot of potential! Ch. Shurlock Holmes O'BJ, owned by Bill and BJ Andrews, at ten weeks of age.

a bright young pup is quite capable of handling more than one command per lesson, and certainly per day. Indeed, as time progresses, you will be going through each command as a matter of routine before a new one is attempted. This is so the puppy always starts, as well as ends, a lesson on a high note, having successfully completed something.

Call the puppy to you and fuss over him. Place one hand on his hindquarters and the other under his upper chest. Say "Sit" in a pleasant (never harsh) voice. At the same time, push down his rear end and push up under his chest. Now lavish praise on the puppy. Repeat this a few times and your pet will get the idea. Once the puppy is in the sit position you will release your hands. At first he will tend to get up, so immediately repeat the exercise. The lesson will end when the pup is in the sit position. When the puppy understands the command, and does it right

TRAINING

away, you can slowly move backwards so that you are a few feet away from him. If he attempts to come to you, simply place him back in the original position and start again. Do not attempt to keep the pup in the sit position for too long. At this age, even a few seconds is a long while and you do not want him to get bored with lessons before he has even begun them.

THE HEEL COMMAND

All dogs should be able to walk nicely on a leash without their owners being involved in a tug-of-war. The heel command will follow leash training. Heel training is best done where you have a wall to one side of you. This will restrict the puppy's lateral movements, so you only have to contend with forward and backward situations. A fence is an alternative, or you can do the lesson in the garage. Again, it is better to do the lesson in private, not on a public sidewalk where there will be many distractions.

With a puppy, there will be no need to use a choke collar as you can be just as effective with a regular one. The leash should be of good length, certainly not too short. You can adjust the space between you, the puppy, and the wall so your pet has only a small amount of room to move sideways. This being so, he will either hang back or pull ahead—the latter is the more desirable state as it indicates a bold pup who is not frightened of you.

Hold the leash in your right hand and pass it through your left. As the puppy moves ahead and strains on the leash, give the leash a quick jerk backwards with your left hand, at the same time saying "Heel." The position you want the pup to be in is such that his chest is level with, or just behind, an imaginary line from your knee. When the puppy is in this position, praise him and begin walking again, and the whole exercise will be repeated. Once the puppy begins to get the message, you can use your left hand to pat the side of your knee so the pup is encouraged to keep close to your side.

It is useful to suddenly do an about-turn when the pup understands the basics. The puppy will now be behind you, so you can pat your knee and say "Heel." As soon as the pup is in the correct position, give him lots of praise. The puppy will now be beginning to associate certain words with certain actions. Whenever he is not in the heel position he will experience displeasure as you jerk the leash, but when he comes alongside you he will

TRAINING

receive praise. Given these two options, he will always prefer the latter—assuming he has no other reason to fear you, which would then create a dilemma in his mind.

Once the lesson has been well learned, then you can adjust your pace from a slow walk to a quick one and the puppy will come to adjust. The slow walk is always the more difficult for most puppies, as they are usually anxious to be on the move.

If you have no wall to walk against then things will be a little more difficult because the pup will tend to wander to his left. This means you need to give lateral jerks as well as bring the pup to your side. End the lesson when the pup is walking nicely beside you. Begin the lesson with a few sit commands (which he understands by now), so you're starting with success and praise. If your puppy is nervous on the leash, you should never drag him to your side as you may see so many other people do (who obviously didn't invest in a good book like you did!). If the pup sits down, call him to your side and give lots of praise. The pup must always come to you because he wants to. If he is dragged to your side he will see you doing the dragging—a big negative. When he races ahead he does not see you jerk the leash, so all he knows is that something restricted his movement and, once he was in a given position, you gave him lots of praise. This is using canine psychology to your advantage.

Always try to remember that if a dog must be disciplined, then try not to let him associate the discipline with you. This is not possible in all matters but, where it is, this is definitely to be preferred.

You must remember that your dog has a "pack" mentality and needs to know that you, the owner, are the dominant figure. "Ziggy" is playfully establishing his dominance over puppy "Punch."

TRAINING

THE STAY COMMAND

This command follows from the sit. Face the puppy and say "Sit." Now step backwards, and as you do, say "Stay." Let the pup remain in the position for only a few seconds before calling him to you and giving lots of praise. Repeat this, but step further back. You do not need to shout at the puppy. Your pet is not deaf; in fact, his hearing is far better than yours. Speak just loudly enough for the pup to hear, yet use a firm voice. You can stretch the word to form a "sta-a-a-y." If the pup gets up and comes to you simply lift him up, place him back in the original position, and start again. As the pup comes to understand the command, you can move further and further back.

The next test is to walk away after placing the pup. This will mean your back is to him, which will tempt him to follow you. Keep an eye over your shoulder, and the minute the pup starts to move, spin around and, using a sterner voice, say either "Sit" or "Stay." If the pup has gotten quite close to you, then, again, return him to the original position.

As the weeks go by you can increase the length of time the pup is left in the stay position—but two to three minutes is quite long enough for a puppy. If your puppy drops into a lying position and is clearly more comfortable, there is nothing wrong with this. Likewise, your pup will want to face the direction in which you walked off. Some trainers will insist that the dog faces the direction he was placed in, regardless of whether you move off on his blind side. I have never believed in this sort of obedience because it has no practical benefit.

The Mini Bull Terrier is extremely trainable and eager to please his master. Ch. Crescent T.K.O. is ready to start his obedience work.

TRAINING

THE DOWN COMMAND

From the puppy's viewpoint, the down command can be one of the more difficult ones to accept. This is because the position is one taken up by a submissive dog in a wild pack situation. A timid dog will roll over—a natural gesture of submission. A bolder pup will want to get up, and might back off, not feeling he should have to submit to this command. He will feel that he is under attack from you and about to be punished—which is what would be the position in his natural environment. Once he comes to understand this is not the case, he will accept this unnatural position without any problem.

Ch. Crescent T.K.O. demonstrates the "sit/stay" command with some of his friends from obedience class.

You may notice that some dogs will sit very quickly, but will respond to the down command more slowly—it is their way of saying that they will obey the command, but under protest!

There are two ways to teach this command. One is, in my mind, more intimidating than the other, but it is up to you to decide which one works best for you. The first method is to stand in front of your puppy and bring him to the sit position, with his collar and leash on. Pass the leash under your left foot so that when you pull on it, the result is that the pup's neck is forced downwards. With your free left hand, push the pup's shoulders down while at the same time saying "Down." This is when a bold pup will instantly try to back off and wriggle in full protest. Hold the pup firmly by the shoulders so he stays in the position for a second or two, then tell him what a good dog he is and give him lots of praise. Repeat this only a few times in a lesson

TRAINING

because otherwise the puppy will get bored and upset over this command. End with an easy command that brings back the pup's confidence.

The second method, and the one I prefer, is done as follows: Stand in front of the pup and then tell him to sit. Now kneel down, which is immediately far less intimidating to the puppy than to have you towering above him. Take each of his front legs and pull them forward, at the same time saying "Down." Release the legs and quickly apply light pressure on the shoulders with your left hand. Then, as quickly, say "Good boy" and give lots of fuss. Repeat two or three times only. The pup will learn over a few lessons. Remember, this is a very submissive act on the pup's behalf, so there is no need to rush matters.

Be consistent with your Mini Bull when enforcing the rules of the household. For example, if you let your dog sleep on the bed when he is younger, it will be harder to break him of the habit later on.

RECALL TO HEEL COMMAND

When your puppy is coming to the heel position from an off-leash situation—such as if he has been running free—he should do this in the correct manner. He should pass behind you and take up his position and then sit. To teach this command, have the pup in front of you in the sit position with his collar and leash on. Hold the leash in your right hand. Give him the command to heel, and pat your left knee. As the pup starts to move forward, use your right hand to guide him behind you. If need be you can hold his collar and walk the dog around the back of you to the desired position. You will need to repeat this a few times until the dog understands what is wanted.

When he has done this a number of times, you can try it without the collar and leash. If the pup comes up toward your left side, then bring him to the sit position in front of you, hold his collar and walk him around the back of you. He will eventually understand and auto-

TRAINING

Well-trained puppies will grow up to be pleasant adults that are welcomed in any home and enjoyed by everyone. Owners, David and Susan Glasgow

matically pass around your back each time. If the dog is already behind you when you recall him, then he should automatically come to your left side, which you will be patting with your hand.

THE NO COMMAND

This is a command that must be obeyed every time without fail. There are no halfway stages, he must be 100-percent reliable. Most delinquent dogs have never been taught this command; included in these are the jumpers, the barkers, and the biters. Were your puppy to approach a poisonous snake or any other potential danger, the no command, coupled with the recall, could save his life. You do not need to give a specific lesson for this command because it will crop up time and again in day-to-day life.

If the puppy is chewing a slipper, you should approach the pup, take hold of the slipper, and say "No" in a stern voice. If he jumps onto the furniture, lift him off and say "No" and place him gently on the floor. You must be consistent in the use of the command and apply it every time he is doing something you do not want him to do.

BREED CONCERNS

This will be a blessedly short chapter. There are some breed related problems such as primary lens luxation (an eye abnormality) and from a breeding standpoint, one may encounter occasional difficulties in mating, whelping, or first-week know how on the part of the mom.

Careful pedigree study and a good working knowledge of genetics will avoid most inherited problems such as lens luxation, slipping patellae, or improper dental occlusion known as a "bad mouth."

Some Mini Bull moms may experience trouble during mating and whelping. This is Elly helping out Gracie by nursing one of Gracie's pups for her.

As for whelping, if a bitch doesn't settle in with the litter within 24 hours, beware. Some females are not meant to reproduce their species. A good Bullie is a devoted, careful, attentive mom with tons of milk and patience. If she's less than that, remove the whelps, hand rear them, and don't breed the bitch again.

On the other hand, if she's had a cesarean section, she's quite likely to experience anything from fear of her newborns, to total apathy, to not knowing exactly what the new things are. Imagine waking up from a frightful nap only to find such odd little creatures attached to your belly!

So, if she's to be sectioned, keep anesthesia to a minimum and please don't fall into the trap of over-sanitizing the newborns. In fact, have the vet preserve some of the placental material, sealing it in a ziplock bag. Upon returning home, warm it to canine body

BREED CONCERNS

temperature (101.5 degrees) under warm water — *not* in the microwave. Then smear the fresh fluids onto the dam's genital area and the new babies. This will likely stimulate her to clean first herself, and then the babies.

The licking impulse, which she has hopefully been allowed to develop during the early stages of labor, is an important bonding mechanism that is all but eliminated by surgical intervention. Depriving the mom of such normal birthing activities creates many unnecessary and avoidable problems.

Generally speaking, the Bull Terrier is as tough as shoe leather, as indestructible as a tank, and cuts or bruises heal with the speed of light! We once had a three-month-old bitch puppy that literally fell *off* of our front yard. It was so steep up on Snob Knob that she rolled perhaps a hundred feet before finally getting herself stopped and right side up. As we scrambled down the embankment to get her, we realized she could not stand. A quick trip to the vet revealed a fractured pelvis and his opinion was that not much could be done. He said it would eventually heal although it would spoil her movement and we need not expect to show her.

Due to careful breeding, the Miniature Bull Terrier has escaped most of the problems that are usually associated with miniature breeds.

BREED CONCERNS

A crew of healthy Miniature Bull Terriers owned by Paul Combs.

We took the baby home and installed her on thick padding in the living room crate. She was exhausted and we thought nothing of it when she immediately nodded off. A few hours later, we woke her to be sure she hadn't expired. She was bright eyed and wagged her tail but refused to move. I lifted her from the crate and carried her outside. Under my steadying hand, she carefully emptied her bladder without squatting. She then stood looking up at me, clearly waiting for me to carry her back inside.

Food and water were served in the crate and other than the essentials of survival with which we assisted her, she slept, scarcely moving, lovely head tucked under her chest in that "I'm hugging myself" position all Bull Terrier owners cherish.

Then, 21 days later, she barked as I passed by her crate. Startled, I turned and she was standing up, wagging, black eyes sparkling with pure Bull Terrier deviltry. "OK," I thought, "she's ready to come out on her own." And that she did, walking ever so slowly, testing the mechanics and flexibility of stiffened joints. At one point, just before we made it to the front door, she paused and looked back at her rear quarters as though to be sure whatever strange sensations she was experiencing came from her own flesh. Satisfied that all was working again, her tail came higher and she looked up at me smiling, pleased with herself. Out she went, squatted in a normal position for the first

BREED CONCERNS

time, and although we kept her crated for another two weeks and limited her normal rambunctious behavior, she never looked back.

Mini Bulls eat anything and like goats, it doesn't usually bother them. One youngster fancied herself as a pack rat, albeit with one uncharacteristic habit. She preferred to swallow her treasures for safekeeping. Every few days she would be forced to regurgitate such prizes as bolts, washers, coins, the tinfoil from cigarette packages, pieces of plastic, and the occa-

Even as a puppy the Mini Bull Terrier lives up to his reputation — tough as nails and sweet as pie at the same time!

sional Unidentified Object. She became known as "the remnant store" because she always carried a good selection of cloth and vinyl fabrics.

Obviously there is no need to discuss special diets. A premium brand of kibble and a tidy share of fresh meat with a bit of vegetables and fruit will do quite well, thank you very much. Seedless grapes are often greeted with the same fervor as might be elicited by a chicken liver sandwich. Male or female, your Mini should be hard muscle though, not fat. A Mini-Bull shaped like a knockwurst is an invitation to health and orthopedic problems. Sweets should be limited to an occasional yogurt or ice cream treat.

YOUR HEALTHY MINIATURE BULL TERRIER

Dogs, like all other animals, are capable of contracting problems and diseases that, in most cases, are easily avoided by sound husbandry—meaning well-bred and well-cared-for animals are less prone to developing diseases and problems than are carelessly bred and neglected animals. Your knowledge of how to avoid problems is far more valuable than all of the books and advice on how to cure them. Respectively, the only person you should listen to about treatment is your vet. Veterinarians don't have all the answers, but at least they are trained to analyze and treat illnesses, and are aware of the full implications of treatments. This does not mean a few old remedies aren't good standbys when all else fails, but in most cases modern science provides the best treatments for disease.

Opposite: A healthy Mini Bull is a happy Mini Bull! Ch. Grayoak Harvetta Wallbanger owned by Paul Combs.

PHYSICAL EXAMS

Your puppy should receive regular physical examinations or check-ups. These come in two forms. One is obviously performed by your vet, and the other is a day-to-day procedure that should be done by you. Apart from the fact the exam will highlight any problem at an early stage, it is an excellent way of socializing the pup to being handled.

To do the physical exam yourself, start at the head and work your way around the body. You are looking for any sign of lesions, or any indication of parasites on the pup. The most common parasites are fleas and ticks.

HEALTH

HEALTH

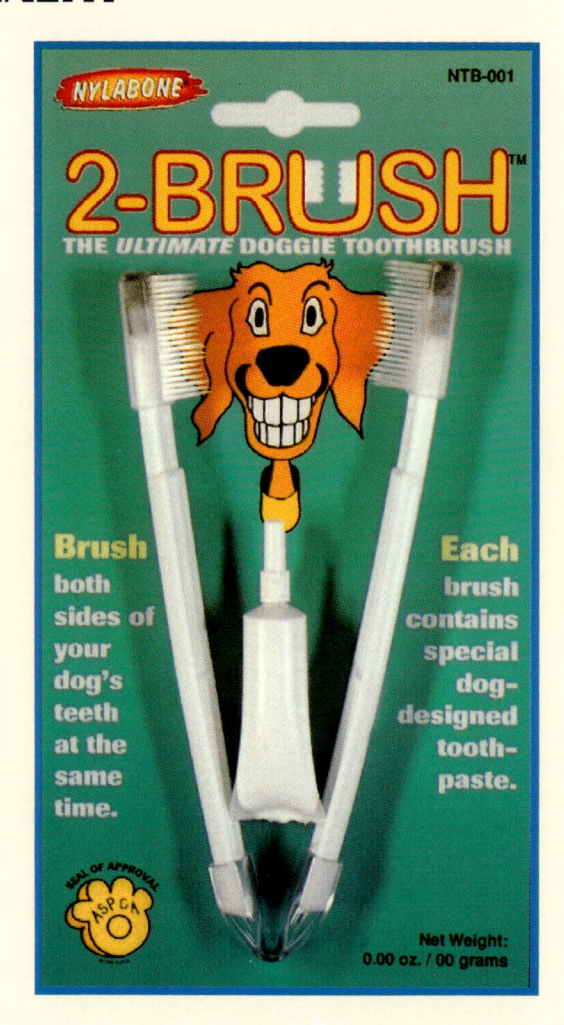

As a pet owner, it is essential to keep your dog's teeth clean by removing surface tartar and plaque. 2-Brush™ by Nylabone® is made with two toothbrushes to clean both sides of your dog's teeth at the same time. Each brush contains a toothpaste reservoir designed to apply the toothpaste, which is specially formulated for dogs, directly into the brush.

HEALTHY TEETH AND GUMS

Chewing is instinctual. Puppies chew so that their teeth and jaws grow strong and healthy as they develop. As the permanent teeth begin to emerge, it is painful and annoying to the puppy, and puppy owners must recognize that their new charges need something safe upon which to chew. Unfortunately, once the puppy's permanent teeth have emerged and settled solidly into the jaw, the chewing instinct does not fade. Adult dogs instinctively need to clean their teeth, massage their gums, and exercise their jaws through chewing.

It is necessary for your dog to have clean teeth. You should take your dog to the veterinarian at least once a year to have his teeth cleaned and to have his mouth examined for any sign of oral disease. Although dogs do not get cavities in the same way humans do, dogs'

HEALTH

The Hercules® by Nylabone® has raised dental tips that help fight plaque on your Miniature Bull Terrier's teeth and gums.

teeth accumulate tartar, and more quickly than humans do! Veterinarians recommend brushing your dog's teeth daily. But who can find time to brush their dog's teeth daily? The accumulation of tartar and plaque on our dog's teeth when not removed can cause irritation and eventually erode the enamel and finally destroy the teeth. Advanced cases, while destroying the teeth, bring on gingivitis and periodontitis, two very serious conditions that can affect the dog's internal organs as well...to say nothing about bad breath!

Since everyone can't brush their dog's teeth daily or get to the veterinarian often enough for him to scale

Nylafloss® does wonders for your Miniature Bull Terrier's dental health by massaging his gums and literally flossing between his teeth, loosening plaque and tartar build-up. Unlike cotton tug toys, Nylafloss® is made from nylon and won't rot or fray.

HEALTH

the dog's teeth, providing the dog with something safe to chew on will help maintain oral hygeine. Chew devices from Nylabone® keep dogs' teeth clean, but they also provide an excellent resource for entertainment and relief of doggie tensions. Nylabone® products give your dog something to do for an hour or two every day and during that hour or two, your dog will be taking an active part in keeping his teeth and gums healthy…without even realizing it! That's invaluable to your dog, and valuable to you!

Nylabone® provides fun bones, challenging bones, and *safe* bones. It is an owner's responsibility to recognize safe chew toys from dangerous ones. Your dog will chew and devour anything you give him. Dogs must not be permitted to chew on items that they can break. Pieces of broken objects can do internal damage to a dog, besides ripping the dog's mouth. Cheap plastic or rubber toys can cause stoppage in the intestines; such stoppages are operable only if caught immediately.

The most obvious choices, in this case, may be the worst choice. Natural beef bones were not designed for chewing and cannot take too much pressure from the sides. Due to the abrasive nature of these bones, they should be offered most sparingly. Knuckle bones, though once very popular for dogs, can be easily

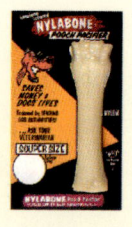

Nylabone®, the only plastic dog bone made of 100% virgin nylon, comes in many different sizes to suit all breeds of dog. The Souper size, shown here, is for larger dogs. Your Mini Bull Terrier, of course, will need the petite size.

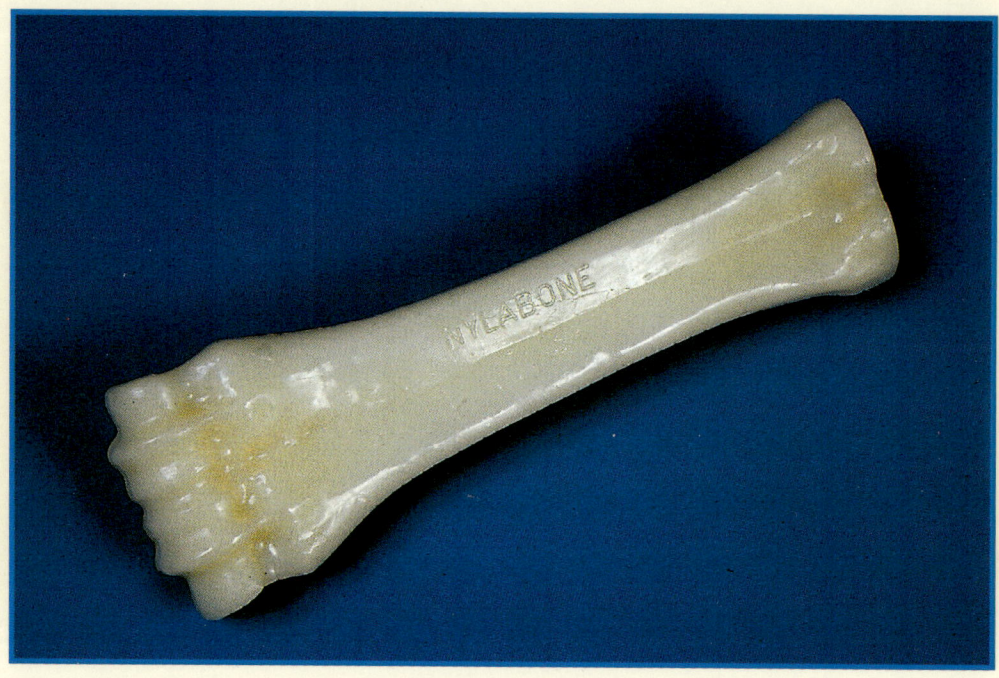

HEALTH

Chick-n-Cheez Chooz® are completely safe and nutritious health chews made from pure cheese protein, chicken, and fortified with vitamin E. They contain no salt, sugar, plastic, or preservatives and less than 1% fat.

chewed up and eaten by dogs. At the very least, digestion is interrupted; at worst, the dog can choke or suffer from intestinal blockage.

When a dog chews hard on a Nylabone®, little bristle-like projections appear on the surface of the bone. These help to clean the dog's teeth and add to the gum-massaging. Given the chemistry of the nylon, the bristle can pass through the dog's intestinal tract without effect. Since nylon is inert, no microorganism can grow on it, and it can be washed in soap and water or sterilized in boiling water or in an autoclave.

For the sake of your dog, his teeth and your own peace of mind, provide your dog with Nylabones®. They have 100 variations from which to choose.

FIGHTING FLEAS

Fleas are very mobile and may be red, black, or brown in color. The adults suck the blood of the host, while the larvae feed on the feces of the adults, which is rich in blood. Flea "dirt" may be seen on the pup as very tiny clusters of blackish specks that look like freshly ground pepper. The eggs of fleas may be laid

HEALTH

on the puppy, though they are more commonly laid off the host in a favorable place, such as the bedding. They normally hatch in 4 to 21 days, depending on the temperature, but they can survive for up to 18 months if temperature conditions are not favorable. The larvae are maggot-like and molt a couple of times before forming pupae, which can survive long periods until the temperature, or the vibration of a nearby host, causes them to emerge and jump on a host.

There are a number of effective treatments available, and you should discuss them with your veterinarian, then follow all instructions for the one you choose. Any treatment will involve a product for your puppy or dog and one for the environment, and will require diligence on your part to treat all areas and thoroughly clean your home and yard until the infestation is eradicated.

THE TROUBLE WITH TICKS

Ticks are arthropods of the spider family, which means they have eight legs (though the larvae have six). They bury their headparts into the host and gorge on its blood. They are easily seen as small grain-like creatures sticking out from the skin. They are often picked up when dogs play in fields, but may also arrive in your yard via wild animals—even birds—or stray cats and dogs. Some ticks are species-specific, others are more adaptable and will host on many species.

The cat flea is the most common flea of dogs. It starts feeding soon after it makes contact with the dog.

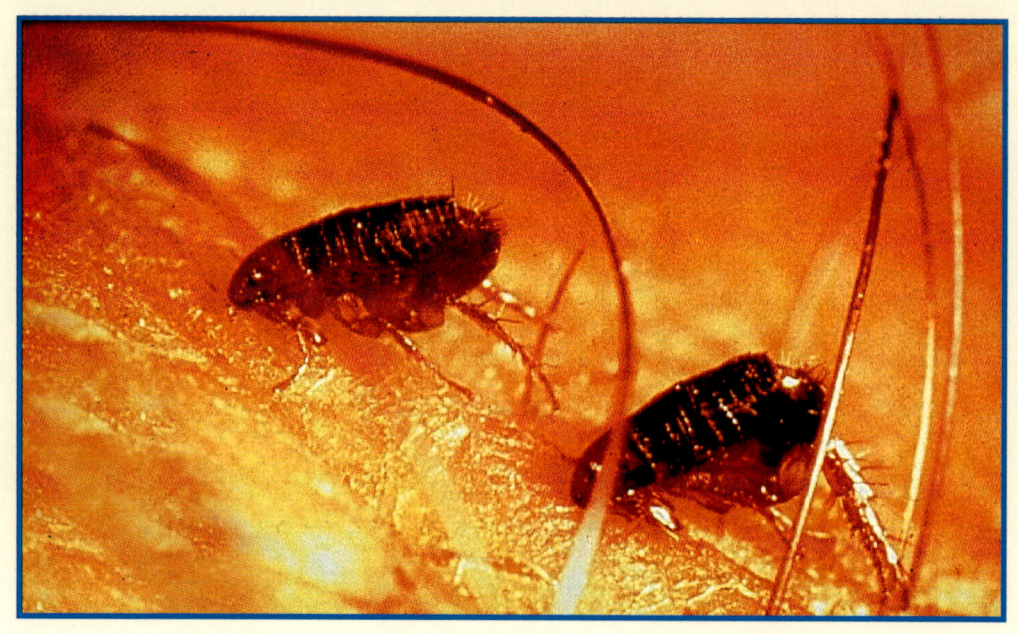

HEALTH

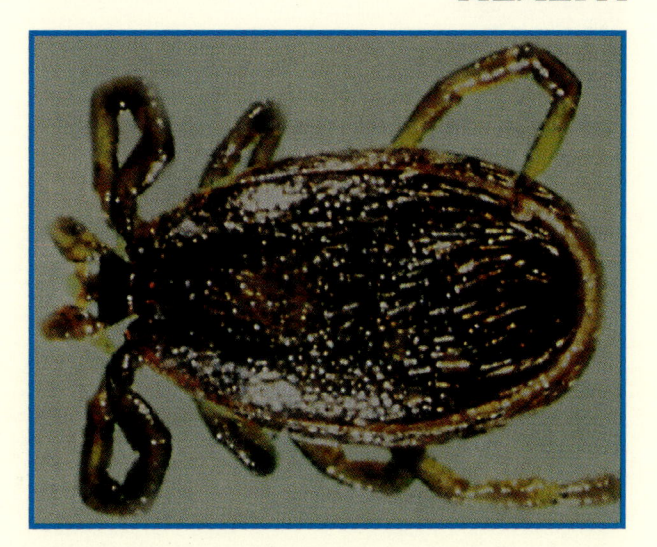

The deer tick is the most common carrier of Lyme disease. Photo courtesy of Virbac Laboratories, Inc., Fort Worth, Texas.

The most troublesome type of tick is the deer tick, which spreads the deadly Lyme disease that can cripple a dog (or a person). Deer ticks are tiny and very hard to detect. Often, by the time they're big enough to notice, they've been feeding on the dog for a few days—long enough to do their damage. Lyme disease was named for the area of the United States in which it was first detected—Lyme, Connecticut—but has now been diagnosed in almost all parts of the U.S. Your veterinarian can advise you of the danger to your dog(s) in your area, and may suggest your dog be vaccinated for Lyme. Always go over your dog with a fine-toothed flea comb when you come in from walking through any area that may harbor deer ticks, and if your dog is acting unusually sluggish or sore, seek veterinary advice.

Attempts to pull a tick free will invariably leave the headpart in the pup, where it will die and cause an infected wound or abscess. The best way to remove ticks is to dab a strong saline solution, iodine, or alcohol on them. This will numb them, causing them to loosen their hold, at which time they can be removed with forceps. The wound can then be cleaned and covered with an antiseptic ointment. If ticks are common in your area, consult with your vet for a suitable pesticide to be used in kennels, on bedding, and on the puppy or dog.

INSECTS AND OTHER OUTDOOR DANGERS

There are many biting insects, such as mosquitoes, that can cause discomfort to a puppy. Many

HEALTH

diseases are transmitted by the males of these species.

A pup can easily get a grass seed or thorn lodged between his pads or in the folds of his ears. These may go unnoticed until an abscess forms.

This is where your daily check of the puppy or dog will do a world of good. If your puppy has been playing in long grass or places where there may be thorns, pine needles, wild animals, or parasites, the check-up is a wise precaution.

SKIN DISORDERS

Apart from problems associated with lesions created by biting pests, a puppy may fall foul to a number of other skin disorders. Examples are ringworm, mange, and eczema. Ringworm is not caused by a worm, but is a fungal infection. It manifests itself as a sore-looking bald circle. If your puppy should have any form of bald patches, let your veterinarian check him over; a microscopic examination can confirm the condition. Many old remedies for ringworm exist, such as iodine, carbolic acid, formalin, and other tinctures, but modern drugs are superior.

When outdoors, Mini Bulls are subject to thorns, ticks, fleas and other dangers. Always check your dog's coat thoroughly after he has been playing outside.

HEALTH

Fungal infections can be very difficult to treat, and even more difficult to eradicate, because of the spores. These can withstand most treatments, other than burning, which is the best thing to do with bedding once the condition has been confirmed.

Mange is a general term that can be applied to many skin conditions where the hair falls out and a flaky crust develops and falls away.

Often, dogs will scratch themselves, and this invariably is worse than the original condition, for it opens lesions that are then subject to viral, fungal, or parasitic attack. The cause of the problem can be various species of mites. These either live on skin debris and the hair follicles, which they destroy, or they bury themselves just beneath the skin and feed on the tissue. Applying general remedies from pet stores is not recommended because it is essential to identify the type of mange before a specific treatment is effective.

Eczema is another non-specific term applied to many skin disorders. The condition can be brought about in many ways. Sunburn, chemicals, allergies to foods, drugs, pollens, and even stress can all produce a deterioration of the skin and coat. Given the range of causal factors, treatment can be difficult because the problem is one of identification. It is a case of taking each possibility at a time and trying to correctly diagnose the matter. If the cause is of a dietary nature then you must remove one item at a time in order to find out if the dog is allergic to a given food. It could, of course, be the lack of a nutrient that is the problem, so if the condition persists, you should consult your veterinarian.

INTERNAL DISORDERS

It cannot be overstressed that it is very foolish to attempt to diagnose an internal disorder without the advice of a veterinarian. Take a relatively common problem such as diarrhea. It might be caused by nothing more serious than the puppy hogging a lot of food or eating something that it has never previously eaten. Conversely, it could be the first indication of a potentially fatal disease. It's up to your veterinarian to make the correct diagnosis.

The following symptoms, especially if they accompany each other or are progressively added to earlier symptoms, mean you should visit the veterinarian right away:

HEALTH

Continual vomiting. All dogs vomit from time to time and this is not necessarily a sign of illness. They will eat grass to induce vomiting. It is a natural cleansing process common to many carnivores. However, continued vomiting is a clear sign of a problem. It may be a blockage in the pup's intestinal tract, it may be induced by worms, or it could be due to any number of diseases.

Diarrhea. This, too, may be nothing more than a temporary condition due to many factors. Even a change of home can induce diarrhea, because this often stresses the pup, and invariably there is some change in the diet. If it persists more than 48 hours then something is amiss. If blood is seen in the feces, waste no time at all in taking the dog to the vet.

Running eyes and/or nose. A pup might have a chill and this will cause the eyes and nose to weep. Again, this should quickly clear up if the puppy is placed in a warm environment and away from any drafts. If it does not, and especially if a mucous discharge is seen, then the pup has an illness that must be diagnosed.

Coughing. Prolonged coughing is a sign of a problem, usually of a respiratory nature.

Wheezing. If the pup has difficulty breathing and makes a wheezing sound when breathing, then something is wrong.

Cries when attempting to defecate or urinate. This might only be a minor problem due to the hard state of the feces, but it could be more serious, especially if the pup cries when urinating.

Cries when touched. Obviously, if you do not handle a puppy with care he might yelp. However, if he cries even when lifted gently, then he has an internal problem that becomes apparent when pressure is applied to a given area of the body. Clearly, this must be diagnosed.

Refuses food. Generally, puppies and dogs are greedy creatures when it comes to feeding time. Some might be more fussy, but none should refuse more than one meal. If they go for a number of hours without showing any interest in their food, then something is not as it should be.

General listlessness. All puppies have their off days when they do not seem their usual cheeky, mischievous selves. If this condition persists for more than two days then there is little doubt of a problem. They may not show any of the signs listed, other than

HEALTH

perhaps a reduced interest in their food. There are many diseases that can develop internally without displaying obvious clinical signs. Blood, fecal, and other tests are needed in order to identify the disorder before it reaches an advanced state that may not be treatable.

WORMS

There are many species of worms, and a number of these live in the tissues of dogs and most other animals. Many create no problem at all, so you are not even aware they exist. Others can be tolerated in small levels, but become a major problem if they number more than a few. The most common types seen in dogs are roundworms and tapeworms. While roundworms are the greater problem, tapeworms require an intermediate host so are more easily eradicated.

Roundworms are spaghetti-like worms that cause a pot-bellied appearance and dull coat, along with more severe symptoms, such as diarrhea and vomiting. Photo courtesy of Merck AgVet.

Roundworms of the species *Toxocara canis* infest the dog. They may grow to a length of 8 inches (20 cm) and look like strings of spaghetti. The worms feed on the digesting food in the pup's intestines. In chronic cases the puppy will become pot-bellied, have diarrhea, and will vomit. Eventually, he will stop eating, having passed through the stage when he always seems hungry. The worms lay eggs in the puppy and these pass out in his feces. They are then either ingested by the pup, or they are eaten by mice, rats, or beetles. These may then be eaten by the puppy and the life cycle is complete.

Larval worms can migrate to the womb of a pregnant bitch, or to her mammary glands, and this is how they pass to the puppy. The pregnant bitch can be wormed, which will help. The pups can, and should,

HEALTH

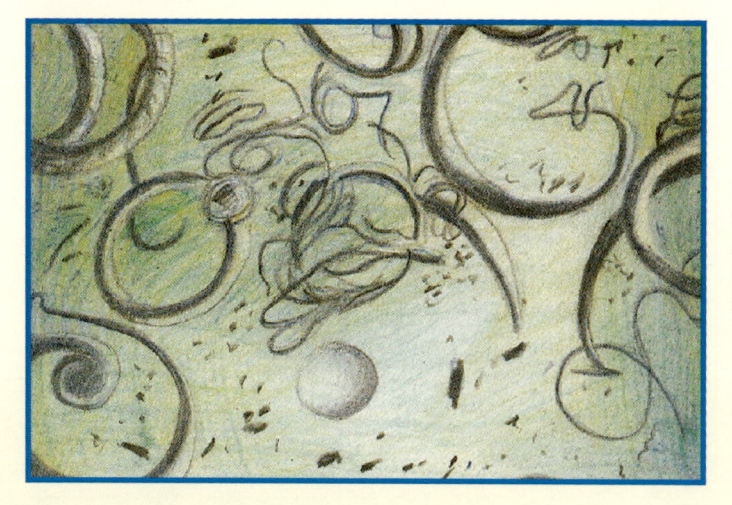

Whipworms are hard to find unless you strain your dog's feces, and this is best left to a veterinarian. Pictured here are adult whipworms.

be wormed when they are about two weeks old. Repeat worming every 10 to 14 days and the parasites should be removed. Worms can be extremely dangerous to young puppies, so you should be sure the pup is wormed as a matter of routine.

Tapeworms can be seen as tiny rice-like eggs sticking to the puppy's or dog's anus. They are less destructive, but still undesirable. The eggs are eaten by mice, fleas, rabbits, and other animals that serve as intermediate hosts. They develop into a larval stage and the host must be eaten by the dog in order to complete the chain. Your vet will supply a suitable remedy if tapeworms are seen or suspected. There are other worms, such as hookworms and whipworms, that are also blood suckers. They will make a pup anemic, and blood might be seen in the feces, which can be examined by the vet to confirm their presence. Cleanliness in all matters is the best preventative measure for all worms.

Heartworm infestation in dogs is passed by mosquitoes but can be prevented by a monthly (or daily) treatment that is given orally. Talk to your vet about the risk of heartworm in your area.

BLOAT (GASTRIC DILATATION)

This condition has proved fatal in many dogs, especially large and deep-chested breeds, such as the Weimaraner and the Great Dane. However, any dog can get bloat. It is caused by swallowing air during exercise, food/water gulping or another strenuous task. As many believe, it is not the result of flatulence. The stomach of an affected dog twists, disallowing

HEALTH

food and blood flow and resulting in harmful toxins being released into the bloodstream. Death can easily follow if the condition goes undetected.

The best preventative measure is not to feed large meals or exercise your puppy or dog immediately after he has eaten. Veterinarians recommend feeding three smaller meals per day in an elevated feeding rack, adding water to dry food to prevent gulping, and not offering water during mealtimes.

VACCINATIONS

Every puppy, purebred or mixed breed, should be vaccinated against the major canine diseases. These are distemper, leptospirosis, hepatitis, and canine parvovirus. Your puppy may have received a temporary vaccination against distemper before you purchased him, but be sure to ask the breeder to be sure.

The age at which vaccinations are given can vary, but will usually be when the pup is 8 to 12 weeks old. By this time any protection given to the pup by antibodies received from his mother via her initial milk feeds will be losing their strength.

The puppy's immune system works on the basis that the white blood cells engulf and render harmless

Rely on your veterinarian for the most effectual vaccination schedule for your Miniature Bull Terrier puppy.

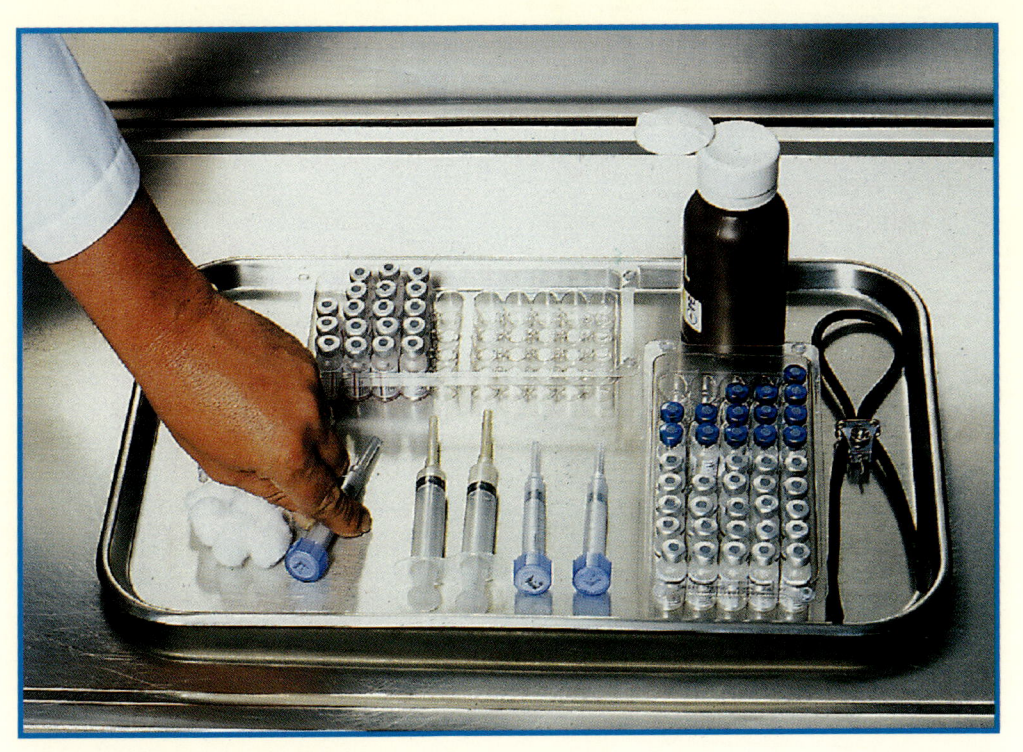

HEALTH

attacking bacteria. However, they must first recognize a potential enemy.

Vaccines are either dead bacteria or they are live, but in very small doses. Either type prompts the pup's defense system to attack them. When a large attack then comes (if it does), the immune system recognizes it and massive numbers of lymphocytes (white blood corpuscles) are mobilized to counter the attack. However, the ability of the cells to recognize these dangerous viruses can diminish over a period of time. It is therefore useful to provide annual reminders about the nature of the enemy. This is done by means of booster injections that keep the immune system on its alert. Immunization is not 100-percent guaranteed to be successful, but is very close. Certainly it is better than giving the puppy no protection.

Dogs are subject to other viral attacks, and if these are of a high-risk factor in your area, then your vet will suggest you have the puppy vaccinated against these as well.

Your puppy or dog should also be vaccinated against the deadly rabies virus. In fact, in many places it is illegal for your dog not to be vaccinated. This is to protect your dog, your family, and the rest of the animal population from this deadly virus that infects the nervous system and causes dementia and death.

ACCIDENTS

All puppies will get their share of bumps and bruises due to the rather energetic way they play. These will usually heal themselves over a few days. Small cuts should be bathed with a suitable disinfectant and then smeared with an antiseptic ointment. If a cut looks more serious, then stem the flow of blood with a towel or makeshift tourniquet and rush the pup to the veterinarian. Never apply so much pressure to the wound that it might restrict the flow of blood to the limb.

In the case of burns you should apply cold water or an ice pack to the surface. If the burn was due to a chemical, then this must be washed away with copious amounts of water. Apply petroleum jelly, or any vegetable oil, to the burn. Trim away the hair if need be. Wrap the dog in a blanket and rush him to the vet. The pup may go into shock, depending on the severity of the burn, and this will result in a lowered blood pressure, which is dangerous and the reason the pup must receive immediate veterinary attention.

HEALTH

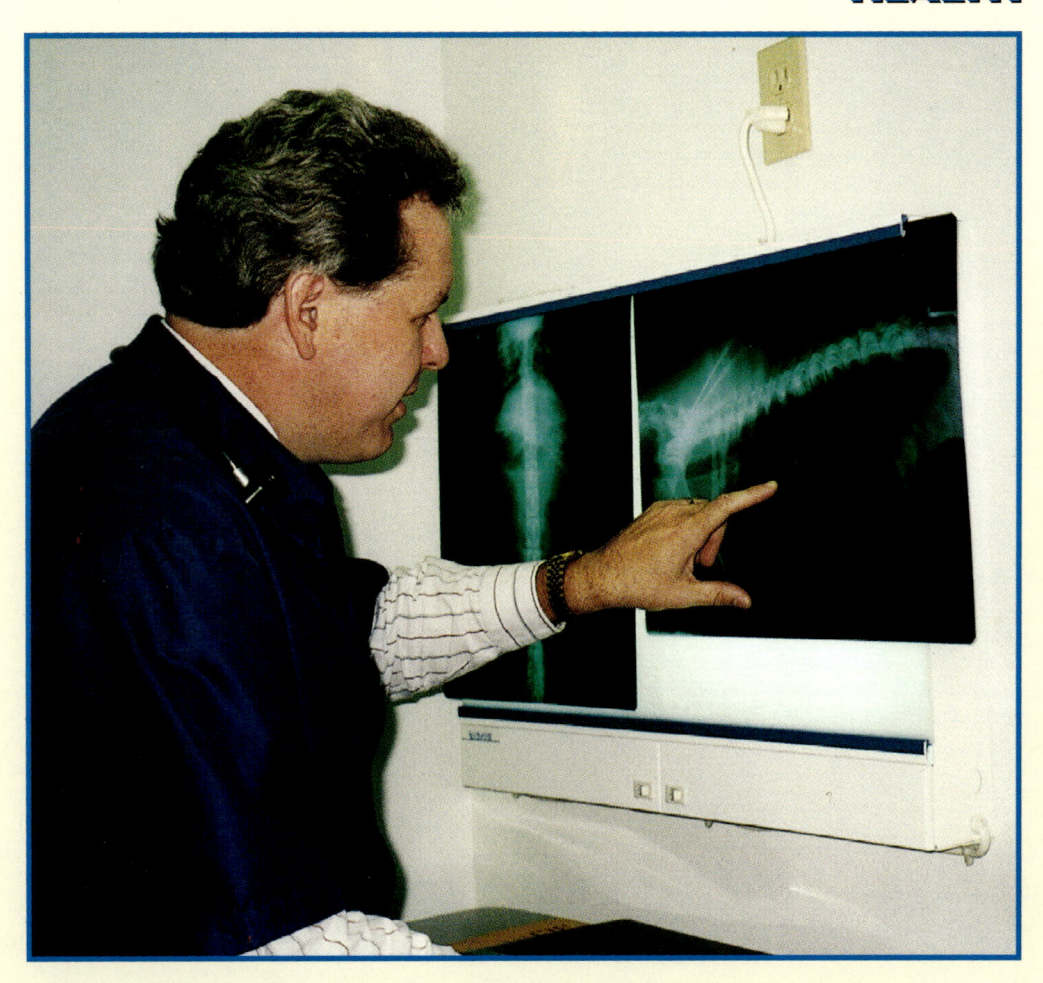

It is a good idea to x-ray the chest and abdomen on any dog hit by a car.

If a broken limb is suspected then try to keep the animal as still as possible. Wrap your pup or dog in a blanket to restrict movement and get him to the veterinarian as soon as possible. Do not move the dog's head so it is tilting backward, as this might result in blood entering the lungs.

Do not let your pup jump up and down from heights, as this can cause considerable shock to the joints. Like all youngsters, puppies do not know when enough is enough, so you must do all their thinking for them.

Provided you apply strict hygiene to all aspects of raising your puppy, and you make daily checks on his physical state, you have done as much as you can to safeguard him during his most vulnerable period. Routine visits to your veterinarian are also recommended, especially while the puppy is under one year of age. The vet may notice something that did not seem important to you.

EARS
Small, thin, placed close together.

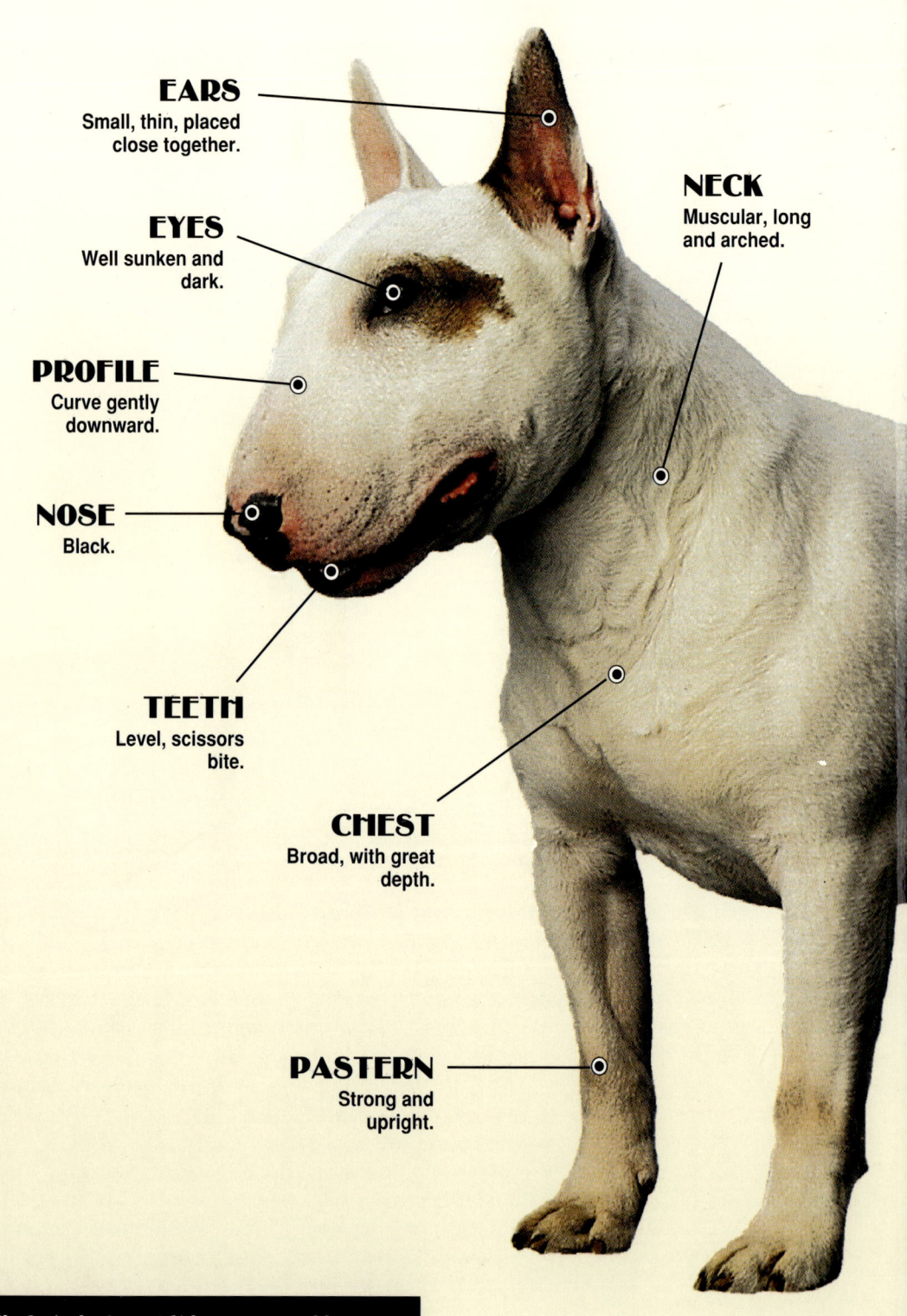

NECK
Muscular, long and arched.

EYES
Well sunken and dark.

PROFILE
Curve gently downward.

NOSE
Black.

TEETH
Level, scissors bite.

CHEST
Broad, with great depth.

PASTERN
Strong and upright.

Ch. Stainsby Soup Of The Day, owned by L. Holland, Dana Cline and B. Wycoff.